THE COYOTES OF CANAAN

THE COYOTES OF CANAAN

EDWIN DARYL MICHAEL

Charleston, West Virginia

Quarrier Press
Charleston, WV

©2021, Edwin Daryl Michael

Other Historical Fiction By Edwin Daryl Michael

Shadow of the Alleghenies
Death Visits Canaan
The Last Appalachian Wolf

Book and cover design: Mark S. Phillips
Cover photograph: © Linda Freshwaters Arndt, freshwaters-arndt.com
Back cover photograph: © John Edwards, WVU

ISBN-13: 978-1-942294-20-7
ISBN-10: 1-942294-20-4

10 9 8 7 6 5 4 3 2 1

Printed in the United States of America

Distributed by:

West Virginia Book Co.
1125 Central Ave.
Charleston, WV 25302
www.wvbookco.com

TABLE OF CONTENTS

FOREWORD

This is a work of fiction. However, all actions and behaviors described herein are based on actual events. Coyote behavior has been intensively studied.

I (the author) reside part time in Canaan Valley, West Virginia, and have conducted wildlife research here for over 45 years. I have had personal encounters with coyotes and interviewed local residents with coyote experiences. My tenure as Professor of Wildlife Management at West Virginia University made possible my familiarity with all coyote research conducted in West Virginia and neighboring states.

All geographical locations mentioned in the novel are real, but any names of people are fictitious.

ACKNOWLEDGMENTS

I am indebted to Julie and Ken Dzaack for their efforts to assure the biological and geographical accuracy of the novel, as well as their encouragement and thoughtful comments in making it more readable.

I am also grateful to Chris Ryan, WVDNR, for his input on bear hounds, and to Rich Rogers, WVDNR, for his assistance in obtaining coyote trapping data.

And, as usual, I leaned heavily on the advice of the Michael Editors to direct the passage of this novel from a rough draft to a polished manuscript.

MAP OF THE CENTRAL APPALACHIAN REGION

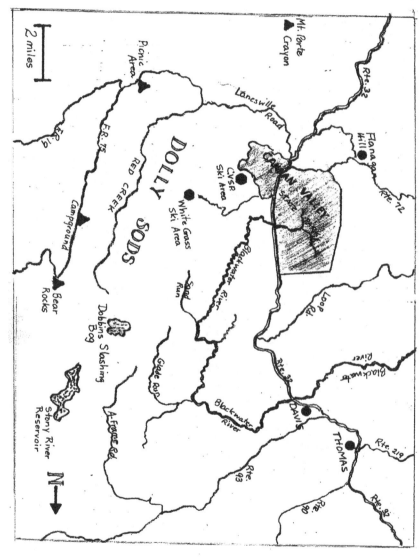

MAP OF CANAAN VALLEY – DOLLY SODS AREA

IN THE BEGINNING

Spring had returned to the Adirondacks. The five small pups were playing outside their den, with no cares in the world—totally unaware of the large timber wolf stealthily inching towards them. They had been born in late April, when scattered drifts of snow lay two feet deep on the hillside above and temperatures hovered around freezing. Temperatures inside the den, however, were close to 50 degrees. The body heat produced by the mother coyote inside a snug den, less than two feet across, created comfortable conditions for the newborns. The narrow width of the twisting, 12-foot long passageway impeded the flow of cold outside air.

The litter of six pups included three males and three females. Each pup weighed about ten ounces. Their soft, wooly, grayish-brown birth hair was quite prominent.

The pups had no difficulty finding one of the eight, milk-engorged teats of the mother. Coyote's eyes are closed at birth, but by their second week, they open. Although bright blue, their eyes would transform to golden-yellow by eight weeks of age.

By week five, the pups had crawled through the meandering tunnel and poked their heads outside, fascinated by the sights and sounds, but not brave enough to venture out. The mating calls of vireos and warblers dominated the aboveground sounds, but in the background were drumming grouse, croaking wood frogs, and scolding red squirrels.

By week ten, they began to venture outside the den. The largest of the male pups was the first to wander short distances. That particular pup, darker in color than the others, was also quite aggressive towards his littermates and was already establishing his dominance.

The mother coyote had begun to leave the den when the pups were eight weeks of age. She would often be away for hours at a time, hunting for food to produce the rich milk so essential for the growth of her pups. She had lost weight while nursing the pups, even though her mate brought food daily.

On a sunny June morning, when the mother was away hunting, the pups had ventured nearly 20 yards from their den. The numerous bones scattered around the opening were fascinating playthings, and unfamiliar odors from nearby fallen trees pulled them like magnets.

They were romping and chasing when the timber wolf appeared some 50 yards away. Topping the knoll that rose a short distance above the den opening, the wolf dropped to his belly and watched the pups intently. He lay motionless for over 15 minutes, then slowly made his way downhill towards the highly vulnerable pups.

The smallest female of the litter had been captured the previous week by a golden eagle, when they were playing outside in bright sunshine. The pups had experienced the first serious fright of their short life when the enormous brown bird with six foot wingspan swooped close to the ground and snatched the pup with its three-inch long talons. She had time for only one short squeal before a talon pierced her heart.

When the wolf was less than 20 yards away, the pups spotted him and scampered into the den—all but the largest male. He had been digging behind a log and had not noticed the approaching canid. Only six feet from the pup, the male wolf crouched and emitted a low growl. The pup poked his head over the log and spotted the wolf. Rather than running for the den entrance, the pup ran directly towards the wolf. Most coyote pups learn early in life a key rule to survival: every living thing smaller than you is something you can eat, while everything larger than you is something that can eat you.

A casual observer would have been dumbfounded to see the pup lick the mouth of the wolf. However, the wolf was the pup's father.

The male wolf and the female coyote had mated the previous February, and this was their first litter. The three-year old female coyote had lived her entire life in the Adirondacks, but the two-year old wolf had been raised in Algonquin Provincial Park, Ontario, Canada.

The wolf's sire, a 125-pound male, had become aggressive towards the male pups of his litter when mating season began in December. On three consecutive days, he drove his male offspring away from his pack's moose-kill, but the juvenile males, each 22 months old, were not overly stressed.

Two of the adolescent males went north, and one sibling wandered into New York. With his advancing sexual maturity, he had begun to feel the urge to mate in a territory of his own. He wandered southeast across the St. Lawrence River in January. The river was frozen over, and the wolf crossed unhampered at the Thousand Islands area, where a string of normally water-bound land masses created a passage.

The distance from Algonquin Park to the Adirondacks was slightly over 200 miles—an insignificant distance for an animal that frequently covered 50 miles in a day. Adirondack State Park provided near optimum habitat for such juvenile male wolves. Encompassing 2.6 million acres owned by the State of New York, it was the largest protected wilderness area east of the Mississippi River. The complex of coniferous and hardwood forests, 3,000 lakes and ponds, plus 30,000 miles of streams and rivers, provided food in the form of deer, hare, and rodents.

The Canadian wolf had picked up the scent of the female coyote shortly after entering the Adirondacks. She had come into heat early in January and emitted a scent designed to attract male coyotes. Instinctively, the male wolf interpreted the scent exactly as had two male coyotes. He followed the scent for three days before encountering the female and her two suitors.

The wolf weighed twice as much as the male coyotes, and he killed one of them by crushing its backbone and spinal cord with a single bite. On the next day the wolf fractured the femur of the other coyote's hind leg and ripped off his ear.

By the fifth day of courting, the female coyote accepted the wolf's advances and mating began. The pair remained together, with frequent coupling, until the female ovulated in early February. The eggs were fertilized, and six coywolf embryos began to develop. Because the pups had resulted from the union of a coyote and wolf, they would be called "coywolves" by mammalogists.

COYOTE–WOLF HISTORY

For readers to understand the significance of coyotes and timber wolves and the ecological role of the resulting coywolves, it is necessary to describe the historical distribution and interaction of these two species during the 1700s and 1800s.

Coyotes in the 1700s were mainly concentrated in deserts and grasslands west of the Mississippi River and east of the Rocky Mountains, and they were referred to as brush wolves or prairie wolves by early fur trappers. Their range extended from Canada to northern Mexico. These dog-like predators occupied less than 25 percent of what would eventually become the lower 48 states.

The earliest known name applied to them originated with the Aztecs, who used the term "coyotl." Over hundreds of years, this name appears to have morphed among inhabitants of Central and South America and Mexico to eventually became "coyote."

The word was typically pronounced "ki-oh-tee", with strong emphasis on the "tee" ending. Lewis and Clark, on their journey of 1804, called it a "prairie wolf." It was called "maheegan" by the Algonquin and Cree, "mohegan" by the Lenape, "mahingan" by the Mohawk, "wahya" by the Cherokee, and "mweewa" by the Shawnee.

Prior to westward expansion in the 1800s, coyotes rarely ventured outside deserts and grasslands because of the threats from wolves. Adult western coyotes typically weighed 25 to 30 pounds, while a gray wolf commonly reached 120 pounds. Of greater significance, wolves were pack animals, often with 10-15 animals running together. In contrast, most coyotes were solitary or lived as a male-female pair. The discovery of a coyote by a pack of wolves, or even by a lone wolf, produced a predictable outcome—death of the hapless coyote.

Deserts and prairies provided optimum habitat for coyotes, which fed primarily on rabbits and rodents. In contrast, forested habitats could not sustain coyote populations because small prey animals were much less common.

Additional limitations were placed on coyote populations by wolves that wandered grasslands following herds of nomadic buffalo. Wolves were highly territorial, defending their home range against other wolves or coyotes. There was seldom direct competition for food between wolves and coyotes, because wolves fed upon buffalo, deer, and elk, while coyotes concentrated on rabbits and rodents. Regardless of limited interactions, the presence of wolves in prairies subsequently resulted in fewer coyotes.

By the early 1900s, conditions for wolves had changed drastically. Their food supply had been reduced significantly. Buffalo had been virtually eliminated, while antelope, deer, and elk numbers were dramatically lowered by hunting. The landscape, which had supported tens of thousands of wolves only a century earlier, was being steadily transformed. Prairies were plowed; forests were logged; and paved roads were sprouting up. Wolves were also being poisoned, trapped, and shot.

By 1900, the gray wolf had been nearly eliminated. A few had managed to survive in upper Minnesota and Wisconsin, but to reliably experience the howl of a gray wolf it was necessary to venture into Alaska or Canada.

The name *timber wolf* is occasionally used to distinguish the eastern wolf from the western or gray wolf; but most mammalogists consider the names timber wolf and gray wolf to be interchangeable. The last timber wolf in the Appalachian Mountains was killed in West Virginia in 1897.

However, a lesser-known species commonly called the red wolf, possibly persisted after that date. It is the smallest of North American wolves, weighing only 40-60 pounds. It resembles a coyote more than a wolf and had previously roamed throughout the southeastern United States.

Biologists debated the status of the red wolf in the late 1900s, with some arguing that the few remaining in Texas, Louisiana, Mississippi, and North Carolina were hybrids resulting from the mating of red wolves and coyotes. DNA analysis confirmed that the few surviving individuals thought to be red wolves were offspring of coyotes and red wolves.

However, this did not refute the original existence of a distinct species. A few red wolves possibly exist today in southeastern swamplands (especially North Carolina), but they play no role with present day eastern coyotes. In spite of efforts to protect and propagate red wolves, all indications are that there will never again be a breeding, sustained population of this close relative of the coyote.

Red wolves were given the scientific name of *Canis rufus*, ("red dog"), while gray wolves were named *Canis lupus*, ("wolf dog") and coyotes, *Canis latrans* ("barking dog"). Taxonomists often designate the offspring of a wolf-coyote mating as *Canis lupus X Canis latrans*. To date, no unique binomial name, as typically given to most species, has been assigned to coywolves by the American Society of Mammalogists. Rather, many mammalogists refer to these hybrids as the eastern coyote or northeastern coyote (*Canis latrans*).

With the elimination of gray wolves, coyotes began to expand. By 1900, coyotes were established throughout the western half of the United States and had even pushed north into Alaska. By the 1930s they had reached New York, and by the 1950s they also resided in Pennsylvania, Vermont, and Maine. By the late 1900s, coyotes were being reported in every contiguous state.

The Appalachian Mountains were one of the last areas to harbor coyotes, but slowly and surely they became established. Their range expansion coincided with the increase of white-tailed deer. The absence of wolves and mountain lions, plus the increased quality and quantity of foods resulting from timber harvest and abandoned farms, produced near optimum habitat for white-tailed deer—and consequently, for coyotes.

As a general rule, mammals occupying the northern portions of a geographic range are significantly larger than those in the southern portions. For example, male white-tailed deer in Texas seldom reach 150 pounds in weight, whereas those living in Minnesota might attain weights of 400 and even 500 pounds.

As coyotes expanded into the northeastern states, they gradually increased in size, with many individuals reaching 50-55 pounds—nearly double that of southwestern coyotes. The size increase was accelerated by occasional matings between wolves and coyotes. The social behavior of these large hybrid coyotes began to resemble that of wolves, and small packs became commonplace—especially during winter months.

Eastern coyotes slowly changed into pack animals, with a male and female pair, offspring of a recent litter, and an occasional two-year old female from an earlier litter. Larger individuals could bring down smaller or injured deer, while packs were able to kill full-grown bucks, especially when deep snows handicapped deer movements. Coordinated attacks by a pack of coyotes, or coywolves, produced more pounds of food per hour of hunting than individuals pursuing rabbits and rodents.

LIFE OF A COYWOLF PUP

The hybrid pups were certainly not the first *Canis lupus X Canis latrans*. Coywolves had been reported in Canada since the late 1990s. And unlike matings between coyotes and domestic dogs, the coywolf offspring were fertile. Coydogs were rarely, if ever, fertile and so their genes were not passed on.

The coywolf pups matured under the protection, nurturing, and training of their parents. They weighed 15 pounds by the age of ten weeks, and had little to fear from any of the Adirondack predators except an occasional golden eagle or large-pawed lynx.

The wolf proved to be a strong, dependable parent. He had hunted alone when the pups were being nursed by the female coyote and returned daily with food for his mate. Snowshoe hares were the most common food fed to the female, although those were supplemented with juvenile deer, red squirrels, and ruffed grouse.

Weaning of the pups was nearly completed by the time they reached eight weeks of age. The process started when the mother began moving away when they attempted to nurse. At seven weeks of age, she began leaving the den and hunting on her own, or with her mate.

The pups were left alone for long periods of time, and spent daylight hours outside the den. Stalking one another and mock fighting occupied much of their time. In this way, the skills to survive were slowly perfected. Red squirrels were chased. Mice, voles, and shrews attracted considerable attention, but only a few careless voles were captured.

While weaning, both parents brought meat back to the voracious pups. The meat could best be described as *processed*. At the kill site, the adults would swallow chunks of meat. When their stomach could hold no more they returned to the den. Begging by the pups, including licking around the parent's mouth, resulted in regurgitation of the warm, stew-like meat. Pups eagerly fought over small chunks and by ten weeks of age, they were completely weaned.

In the next phase of development, the parents brought back whole animals or large parts such as a deer leg. The most abundant wolf food in the Adirondacks during summer was the snowshoe hare. These large-footed rabbits, which turned white in winter and brown in summer, weighed close to four pounds, providing plenty of nourishment for pups.

Three hare litters, each consisting of two to four young called leverets, were produced each summer. The young hares were born fully furred, with eyes open, and capable of running and jumping a few hours after birth. The young hares spent their early lives above ground—not in underground dens. Although the pups were not capable of catching hares, by September they were catching voles and chipmunks.

With this feeding regimen, the pups closely resembled adult coyotes by October, when they each weighed over 30 pounds. One evening, as heavy, wet snowflakes fell, the parents called to the pups, and they departed on their nightly hunt. Till then, the parents had growled at the pups as they departed, warning them not to follow. The warnings were reinforced by painful nips to the rump when a pup was overly persistent to join.

The largest and most aggressive of the pups was running close behind his mother as the pack stretched out into a single file. However, Adirondus, as we shall henceforth refer to this over-ambitious pup, struggled to keep up with his parents, and emitted an anxious whine when they passed out of sight over a small knoll. His trailing littermates came to a halt upon reaching Adirondus, and all began to whine nervously. Neither parent returned to the pups, but both emitted coaxing calls. The pups soon resumed their pursuit and joined the parents who sat patiently along a small stream.

The male wolf led his small pack along a meandering creek until they reached the base of a dam. The dam was nearly 30 yards in length, and behind it spread a pond covering two acres. Two years earlier, a pair of beavers had cut several hundred big-tooth aspen trees and hauled sections of them from the surrounding hillside to their engineering project.

After months of work, the dam was strong enough and the pond deep enough for them. A lodge was constructed in the deepest section, using short lengths of aspen logs and bushels of mud. The log home provided security for the two beavers during the coming winter and a relatively dry and warm den to give birth to a litter of four beaver kits the following April.

Their first litter had remained for 18 months, then left the pond to start families of their own. The female beaver gave birth to her second litter of kits at about the same time the coywolf pups had been born. On that specific day, when the coywolf pups were accompanying their parents on their first hunt, the young beaver were also assisting their parents.

Beaver are vegetarians, with the succulent bark of aspen trees providing nourishment throughout the year. During spring, summer, and fall, beavers cut down aspen trees with their large orange incisor teeth, divide the fallen log into sections, and then haul those sections to the safety of their pond. There they peel off manageable sections of the bark, chew it with their flattened molars, and utilize the remaining stripped log section to reinforce the lodge and the dam.

Because of snow in winter, the beavers create a food cache on the bottom of their pond. The food cache resembles a haystack constructed of tree branches. When the surface of the pond is frozen, beavers exit through a small hole created in the floor of the lodge, which sits a few feet above water level. They swim to the food cache and select small sections of aspen limbs, which are hauled to the lodge where the large rodents can safely enjoy a nourishing meal.

The creation of a food cache is dependent upon having a deep pond, which is itself dependent upon constructing a solid dam. No other mammal in North America is such an accomplished engineer as the beaver.

As a result, the landscape of Adirondack Park was shaped more by beaver than by any other animal. Hundreds of species of insects, fish, amphibians, reptiles, birds, and mammals were dependent on beaver ponds for their existence.

The male wolf led his pack around the edge of the dam, and then along the edge of the pond. He slowly worked around the stumps of cut aspen trees and through buttonbush, speckled alder, and viburnum bushes that had begun growing when sunlight reached the damp fertile soil.

The wolf was familiar with the habits of beaver. With the assistance of his mate, he had ambushed one of the 50-pound rodents in September when it was cutting aspen. After eating nearly one fourth of it, they made three trips to carry the remainder back to their pups. The fatty flesh had provided multiple meals for the entire family.

With their food cache not yet large enough for winter, the beaver family spent every night on the hillside. The wolf caught the lingering odor of a beaver that had been repairing a small leak in the dam earlier in the evening, but made no effort to cross the dam. Earlier in the summer, he had lost his footing along the slippery mud, logs, and running water, and had no desire to risk another tumble off the dam.

Once their food cache was completed, beaver would spend nearly 24 hours a day ensconced within their fortress-like lodge. During summer the lodge had a moat-like body of water surrounding it, forcing predators to swim across several yards of open water before they could climb atop the lodge. Few attempted the herculean task of digging through the top of a beaver lodge, even with the scent of kits below. Even more daunting, when predators could walk across ice to the lodge, the frozen mud used to reinforce and insulate the lodge was as impenetrable as concrete.

On that October evening, the beavers were busy felling aspen, cutting them into manageable sections, hauling them to the pond, and under water to their food cache. The wolf recognized the sounds of a gnawing beaver and began a low-crouching stalk that would place him between the beaver and the open water. The coyote moved parallel to her mate. That strategy had been perfected during hundreds of previous hunts. Adirondus followed a few yards behind while the other pups anxiously remained together along the shore.

An adult 50-pound beaver was too large for most predators to easily kill, and few bothered trying. Black bears could kill them, but rarely wasted time hunting them. Lynx, bobcats, fisher, and even coyotes did not risk a serious puncture wound from the sharp incisors of a beaver. At 110 pounds, however, a timber wolf could kill a beaver if it could ambush it before it reached the safety of deep water.

When the wolf closed to within 20 yards of the gnawing beaver, the 60-foot aspen tree slowly began wavering. The beaver made one last cut, waddled back a few paces, and watched with confidence as the aspen crashed to the ground. It narrowly missed Adirondus, who yipped in surprise. The tree distracted him, but he recovered quickly and dashed toward the beaver.

The startled beaver tried instinctively to bite the adult wolf, who grabbed the helpless rodent around the back of the neck and punctured it's thick skin. The female coyote grabbed a hind leg. Adirondus, with an excited yip, plunged his teeth into the flat, scaly tail.

Adirondus had just experienced his first kill and taste of warm salty blood. The beaver provided nearly five pounds of flesh for each pack member, and in less than two hours the pups were fighting over bones and pieces of hide while the adults rested nearby. The family did not return to the rest area they had frequented the past two months, but spent the night and all of the next day sleeping in a small stand of balsam fir.

Following his pairing with the female coyote, the wolf had established a territory, which he fiercely defended against all coyotes and wolves. Boundaries of the 15-square-mile area were distinctly marked by urine squirts, fecal droppings, and frequent howls, and only the most ignorant canine would risk death by crossing them.

During the remainder of October and much of November, the pack trotted relentlessly throughout the entire territory, often covering 15 miles a day. They ambushed another beaver, eight snowshoe hares, and found a dead white-tailed deer not recovered by human hunters. They also killed a careless young raccoon searching for wild grapes.

In addition, they had an unfortunate experience with a porcupine. While separated from his pack, one of Adirondus' brothers encountered the clumsy, bark-eating rodent. He attacked the quilled mammal and clamped his jaws around its head. Excruciating pain coursed through his mouth, followed by panicked yelps.

The pack had not previously confronted a porcupine. At 26 pounds, they would make an excellent meal, but only if the pack knew enough to roll them onto their back and bite their exposed belly. Barbed quills from a porcupine penetrate deep enough into the mouth of a predator that they cannot be removed. The young coywolf pawed at the painful quills with no success. The rest of the pack heard his agonizing howls and came to his rescue but there was nothing they could do.

As a juvenile, the mother had recovered from a dozen or so quills that penetrated her face, but none were inside her mouth. Most broke off after a few days and caused infection and considerable pain. However, she eventually recovered.

Her youngster would not be so fortunate. Many of the quills became buried in his tongue, and a few penetrated the roof of his mouth and sinus cavities. The pain was so great that he could not eat, and by early December, the pup no longer accompanied the pack on nightly hunts. Death crept in slowly over three weeks, and by the middle of December, the pack lost him.

Towards the middle of December, Adirondus participated in his first kill of an adult deer. The pack had not eaten in three days, and were getting desperate when they surprised a deer. The snow had drifted up to three feet, and the young doe was struggling as her small hooves sank deeply into the snow.

The coywolf pack managed to remain atop the frozen snow. The chase covered 80 yards before the deer became entangled in the branches of several black spruce trees and fell awkwardly. The wolf closed quickly and clamped his jaws around the neck of the floundering doe. The 50-pound Adirondus arrived next and clamped his jaws around her hind leg.

Instinctively, Adirondus tore through the soft underbelly skin and was rewarded by the taste of warm blood. Raw flesh from the inside of the hindquarter was removed in large chunks and in less than 15 minutes, the innards were exposed. Adirondus inserted his snout inside the steaming cavity and gripped the large mass of intestines. The feel and flavor were not as attractive as chunks of flesh, but the famished coywolf pulled in stiff-legged jerks. In this manner, they were slowly exhumed from the body cavity, exposing the juicy liver and kidneys.

Weighing 155 pounds, the doe provided more meat than the pack could immediately consume. When their hunger was satiated that night, the wolf led them to a nearby open stand of aspen where they licked and preened their fur before falling asleep. They remained in a near-comatose state throughout much of the following day. Late the next evening, the juveniles awoke and returned to the carcass. With no competition from their parents, the coywolves again filled their bellies. The pack remained nearby for two more nights, till little remained other than bones, hide, and intestines.

December and January passed with long nights and deepening snows. The pack, aided rather than harmed by the wintry conditions, killed four more deer and remained in good health.

By February, the female once again entered estrus ("heat"), and the wolf behaved aggressively towards his male offspring. The coywolf juveniles did not understand the strange behavior of their parents. Being wolf-coyote hybrids, they were not sufficiently mature to breed. Whereas juvenile coyotes in the western and southern states reached sexual maturity by the age of ten months, those in the northeast did not reach maturity until nearly 20 months old. A few coywolf males did not reach maturity until at least two years old.

The pack continued to hunt together during the mating process, but by late April the female coyote had selected a den site, and another litter of coywolf pups entered the world. The year-old juveniles were curious, but were not permitted to enter the den. The male wolf hunted with his offspring, but they seldom ventured more than four or five miles from the den.

The new litter of pups matured, and by June all were venturing outside the den. One of the female juveniles, now weighing 45 pounds and larger than her coyote mother, remained at the den "babysitting" the pups while the mother began hunting on her own. Both the mother and father brought food to their five pups and to this juvenile female, whose instinct to care for pups overpowered her own instinct to hunt.

Summer witnessed the deaths of two pups: one due to an attack by a bobcat and the other by drowning in the mucky mud of a deserted, half-drained beaver pond. By October the male wolf, his coyote mate, the four yearlings, and the three surviving current year pups began hunting together.

The nearly four-year-old wolf was an excellent leader, and by December, the pack rarely went more than two days without killing snowshoe hares, a beaver, or a deer. Because of the added size of the pack, they expanded the size of their hunting territory to cover nearly 40 square miles.

In early winter, a new urge began to affect the behavior of Adirondus and his brother, Aldona. Their dedication to the pack began to wane and on some days they hunted separately from the others. In early January, the two young coywolves struck out in a southerly direction and left their old home range. The two did not contemplate leaving, and were unaware they would never again see their family. They were simply following the ever-present nomadic urge. The bachelor brothers instinctively sought habitat where they could establish their own territories—and ultimately their own packs.

The Appalachian Chain

As the brothers left Adirondack Park they encountered roads, farms, and humans. Instinctively, they avoided farms with their strange odors, but they were puzzled by the roads. Fortunately, they encountered dirt roads before the more dangerous paved roads.

The sounds of vehicles on the dirt roads were so disturbing that the coywolf brothers temporarily retreated. Initially, they crouched in the nearby brush and watched vehicles pass before venturing onto a dirt road. After no adverse experiences with dirt roads and vehicles, they slowly began tolerating the sights, sounds, and smells of passing vehicles.

While growing up in Adirondack Park, the brothers had not encountered paved roads, but were familiar with ATVs and snowmobiles. More than 1,000 miles of snowmobile trails snaked through the park, and the pack utilized the trails on many of their nightly hunts. Their mother had lived her entire life in Adirondack Park and had adapted to the vehicles. Her own mother had taught her to move off the trails to safely observe the noisy contraptions.

The mother coyote taught her family to utilize the firm, sunken paths of snowmobiles traveling in deep snow. When the family discovered deer using a snowmobile trail, which happened when snowdrifts made travel difficult, they took advantage and frequently brought down the isolated animals.

East of Utica the brothers encountered a formidable barrier: Interstate I-90. It was early evening when they reached the four-lane highway. They crouched anxiously in a thick stand of spruce, watching as vehicle after vehicle roared past. Trees in the narrow strip of wooded median seemed to offer safety, so when several minutes passed with no vehicles in view, Adirondus dashed across the two west-bound lanes into the wooded median. There he stopped beside a downed larch tree as a tractor-trailer rig roared behind him.

Aldona followed closely behind, but instead of stopping in the median, he continued, disoriented and anxious, into the east-bound lanes of I-90. A Dodge Ram pickup struck him, and the coyote was flung onto the berm. Adirondus watched as the pickup stopped nearly 100 yards down the road and the driver walked back to the coywolf. He hefted the 50-pound animal by its hind legs and carried it to his truck. He awkwardly swung the carcass into his pickup, retrieved his camera from the cab, and snapped several photographs of the animal.

Adirondus trembled nervously as he watched the man. A low growl escaped his throat, and he edged towards the perimeter of the wooded median until he was within two yards of the paved berm. He watched intently as the driver pulled away. Nearly an hour later, after dark, Adirondus safely dashed across the east-bound lanes.

For the first time in his life, Adirondus was alone. While coyotes are typically solitary animals, timber wolves are pack animals. The collective social lives of individuals within a wolf pack provide comfort, as well as successful hunting. Adirondus carried enough wolf DNA that he felt nervous and somewhat frightened about being alone.

Adirondus wandered southwest for the next few days. Eventually he entered the hemlock/white pine forests of Connecticut Hills Wildlife Management Area. Along the way, he encountered another interstate, I-81. Most canids are fairly intelligent and learn from experiences. Adirondus now associated the death of his brother with these roads.

Burned into his memory was the sight of a human carrying his brother and depositing him in the bed of his pickup truck.

Unbeknownst to him, he was destined to encounter numerous highways and thousands of humans. Most wild animals face countless, potentially fatal experiences. Learning and luck enable a few cunning individuals to live to old age.

Adirondus passed south of the Finger Lakes, spent a day in Watkins Glen State Forest, and eventually crossed into Pennsylvania. He had several encounters with livestock, but never was drawn to attack the unfamiliar livestock for food.

In Pennsylvania, another male coywolf was establishing his territory directly in the path of the solitary brother. This male had been born just outside the southeastern corner of Adirondack Park, and had traveled over much the same route as Adirondus. He had mated with a large female coyote the previous January. That pairing resulted in a litter of five pups being produced in April, but none of the pups survived.

A turkey hunter discovered the den one day when the mother coyote was hunting. He spotted the small playful pups and cautiously crawled to within 40 yards. The man had witnessed a coyote killing a young doe the previous winter and vowed to kill every coyote he encountered. Unable to kill a buck during rifle season, he believed coyotes were responsible for his failure. Thereafter, he began carrying carbon monoxide gas cartridges, hoping to locate a coyote den.

The hunter killed one small pup with a blast from his 12-gauge shotgun, then ran rapidly toward the den opening into which the pups had disappeared. Eagerly pulling one of the carbon monoxide gas cartridges from his hunting coat, he ignited the end and thrust it into the den entrance as far as his arm would reach. By stuffing leaves and sticks and soil into the opening, he prevented the toxic gases from escaping the den. The female coyote discovered the plugged den when she returned, and after excavating the tunnel, she found her dead litter.

The parents remained paired and hunted together following the death of their pups. The coywolf had a strong drive to be a member of a pack, and constantly reinforced the bond between the two.

When Adirondus entered the territory, the other coywolf launched a vicious surprise attack. The adult opened his jaws wide, displayed his teeth, hunched his back, and tucked his tail between his legs—an obvious antagonistic posture. Although Adirondus weighed nearly as much as the 60-pound adult coywolf, he had little experience fighting and quickly retreated. An individual defending his territory always has an advantage. Adirondus covered nearly two miles running at top speed before stopping.

Continuing in a southwesterly direction, his wanderlust eventually brought Adirondus to the Appalachian Mountains. As they curve gently towards the south, the ridges provide natural corridors for wandering wildlife to follow. Thus, Adirondus was drawn down the spine of the Appalachians, remaining west of State College, Altoona, and Bedford.

Trotting along a ridge top, Adirondus gradually became aware of a new and strange whirling sound. He detected no odors to identify the source of the eerie sound. As his anxiety and nervousness increased to the point where he was ready to change direction, a shiny object appeared through the tree canopy. Now that he had spotted the source of the sound, he no longer had the fear of the unknown. As he rounded a small bend, a huge 200-foot tall, silvery cylinder came into view. Atop the tall cylinder rotated three blades, each over 100 feet in length. Thus, Adirondus met his first commercial wind turbine.

This was the first of five wind farms that he would encounter in Pennsylvania. The high elevation and the north-south orientation of the ridges provided optimum locations for turbines. Each wind farm contained as many as 16 turbines and provided clean electricity for thousands of homes.

Wildlife were common along the dirt roads that connected the turbines, and Adirondus capitalized on this. The soft soil of the dirt road muffled his steps, giving him a nice advantage on prey as well.

Covering as many as 50 miles a day, he crossed the Pennsylvania Turnpike and then the state line into Maryland. West of Cumberland, Adirondus safely slipped across the train tracks of the Western Maryland Scenic Railway and then across I-68, before entering Savage River State Forest. The next night he continued southwest along the mountains paralleling the North Branch Potomac River, which formed the boundary between Maryland and West Virginia.

Only a year before, a coywolf had entered West Virginia, following much the same route as Adirondus. That wanderer had met an untimely death, being shot by a deer hunter near Short Gap.

Juvenile males of large and mid-sized predators are known to travel unbelievably long distances to find a territory of their own. Perhaps the most spectacular trip documented for a land mammal in North America involved a two-year-old male cougar (mountain lion) in 2009. Born in the Black Hills of South Dakota, this cat headed east, crossing Minnesota and Michigan, then wandering through Ontario and New York. Nearly two years after beginning his journey he reached Connecticut. Unfortunately, his journey came to an abrupt end when a woman ran over him with her car. He had covered at least 2,000 miles.

Similarly impressive was a grizzly bear covering over 2,800 miles between Canada and the Rocky Mountains in the United States during 2006-2013. Gray wolves are known to have dispersed distances as great as 700 miles from their birth site, and juvenile coyotes regularly disperse more than 100 miles. A coywolf traveling from Adirondack Park in New York to Cheat Mountain in West Virginia would cover slightly more than 400 miles.

Male wolf-coyote hybrids in the Adirondacks moved great distances to eventually find a mate. Adirondus met several coyotes as he wandered through New York. Upon meeting Adirondus, those smaller coyotes retreated and he had no reason to pursue them. He also wandered into the territory of a pair of coyotes. Although much smaller than Adirondus, they easily drove him from their territory. Defending one's territory provides an extra incentive while the transient has little reason to fight. Adirondus also encountered two juvenile female coyotes, but they were not yet in heat and proffered no attraction for him.

In Potter County, Pennsylvania, Adirondus had picked up the scent of a coyote-like canine and followed it for several hours. Shortly after midnight, the large coyote became aware of the much larger coywolf. Adirondus weighed over 65 pounds, and stood nearly 27 inches tall at the shoulders. His impressive body was 50 inches long, and his brushy tail added another 15 inches. Although frightened, the coyote did not retreat. He had lost his mate of five years in December, and was obviously searching for a companion.

The two approached cautiously, and the coyote rolled onto his back in a gesture of submission and friendship. Adirondus sniffed carefully, before nipping playfully at the coyote's rump. In a few hours, the two were hunting together. That evening they discovered an adult doe which had been wounded by a hunter. It had died in a thick patch of rhododendron two weeks after being shot, and had been discovered by a pair of bobcats. The felines ate a couple meals and then covered the carcass with leaves and twigs, before searching for fresh meat.

Adirondus and his companion remained near the carcass for four days. Two days later, they were foraging along the edge of a pasture in search of cottontail rabbits, whose scent was scattered through the blackberry thicket bordering a barbed wire fence. Unbeknownst to them, a dairy farmer was repairing a nearby section of fence. His John Deere tractor was parked along the fence as he strung a new strand of barbed wire between the adjoining fence posts.

The farmer had shut off the tractor and was leaning against a large tire when he spotted the two canines. The mismatched pair had topped over a small knoll, intent on the fresh scent left by a cottontail rabbit. The farmer had lost several of his free-ranging turkeys the previous October, and he suspected a fox, bobcat, or coyote. Slowly reaching into the cab of his tractor, he retrieved his double-barrel Ithaca shotgun, which was loaded with double "OO" buckshot for just such opportunities. The two shotgun shells each held 12 lead pellets, each about the size of a small green pea.

With the prevailing winds coming from behind them, the scent of the human and his tractor did not reach the coywolf and coyote. The farmer waited until the two were close together before leveling the shotgun sights on the smaller of the two. He squeezed the right trigger. Almost immediately he moved the sights onto the scurrying larger animal, quickly pulling the old gun's left trigger. At the sound of the first exploding shell, Adirondus had leapt to his left towards the protection of the woodlot. Twelve, pea-sized pellets now flew through the air towards him.

Designed for duck hunting, the farmer's shotgun offered a right barrel choked to throw a tight pattern, while the left barrel was choked to throw a slightly wider, less dense pattern. At least six of the double "00" shot struck the old coyote behind the shoulder and he ran only a few yards before collapsing. One pellet from the second shell struck Adirondus in the left hip, but stopped in the muscle before doing damage to a bone.

The coyote died almost immediately, but Adirondus burst from the field and out of sight. Running frantically, he sprinted 250 yards before stopping. Pain began to course through his leg as he experienced his first gunshot wound.

Adirondus had spotted the farmer when the gunpowder exploded and immediately associated him with the sound, and now with the pain in his left hip. Also seared in the depths of his mind were the sight of the bright green tractor and the smell of cow manure.

Adirondus slowly recovered from his shotgun wound during the next two weeks, and by the time he entered West Virginia the pain had almost completely disappeared.

ALLEGHENY FRONT AND DOLLY SODS

Adirondus crossed the North Branch River just upstream of Keyser, West Virginia, and resumed his southward trek down the spine of the Appalachians. A day later he encountered another row of wind turbines. The coywolf had reached the northernmost tower in a string of 132 turbines that stretched nearly 12 miles. He followed the windmills along the dirt road connecting them, feeding on deer, rabbits, and rodents.

Adirondus continued to follow the whirling turbines, the night winds making them produce a low-pitched "whoosh" overhead. By midmorning, he reached the end of the turbines.

Rather than hardwood forests dominated by oak trees, a diversity of habitats similar to those he had experienced as a youngster spread out before him. Scattered stands of red spruce trees, often as small as one acre, were interspersed among shrubby stands of rhododendron, mountain laurel, and blueberry. Broad expanses of low-growing ferns and grasses were also abundant.

Of greatest interest within the rolling hills were numerous wetlands. Alder thickets and bogs of cranberry and sphagnum moss made the plateau even more promising. Scattered along streams were numerous beaver ponds. Much of the coywolf's hunting territory during the following month centered on the Old Stony River Reservoir. Adirondus spent hours sitting on exposed knolls studying the landscape that spread before him—triggering memories of the land he had known as a pup.

Adirondus' hunts brought him to a prominent formation of large boulders at the edge of a sharp drop off to the east. This formation was called Bear Rocks. In reality, the ten acres of pickup truck sized, sandstone boulders were less apt to be visited by bears than by people. During late summer and early fall, the site attracted thousands who were interested in picking blueberries and enjoying the spectacular view to the east.

Adirondus' travels were pulling him down the Allegheny Plateau. It extends mostly unnoticed for almost 180 miles from south-central Pennsylvania into West Virginia, but becomes quite distinct in Grant and Tucker counties in West Virginia. The eastern border of the Plateau, known as the Allegheny Front, consists of a steep, escarpment of sandstone/conglomerate rock—often two to three miles wide. The Allegheny Front lies at about 4,000 feet elevation here, but drops as much as 2,000 feet to the South Branch River.

The Allegheny Front forms the Eastern Continental Divide along much of its length. Most rain falling on the plateau flows westward into the Cheat River Drainage, before flowing north into the Monongahela River, then farther north to the Forks of the Ohio, south to the Mississippi, and then a final 1,000 miles to the Gulf of Mexico. In contrast, rain falling east of the Allegheny Front flows eastward into the tributaries of the Potomac River. These, in turn, eventually enter the Chesapeake Bay as it merges with the Atlantic Ocean.

None of this hydrology was important to Adirondus. He had this section of the Allegheny Plateau, known as Dolly Sods, to satisfy his search for food. With a width of nearly four miles and a length of over ten miles, Dolly Sods sits high above the surrounding lands—a relatively flat 26,000 acre plateau.

A major chunk of the plateau, the 17,371-acre Dolly Sods Wilderness, provided a great variety of habitat types and a diversity of animals. And humans were nearly nonexistent at that time of the year.

Most of the Dolly Sods plateau falls within the Monongahela National Forest, and Forest Service Road 75, which provides access for hikers, campers, and blueberry pickers during summer months, remains closed all winter due to deep snows.

Despite the closure, humans are not entirely absent. Adirondus spotted a trio of cross-country skiers after he had reached Bear Rocks. He had been sleeping, curled into a ball at the edge of a red spruce stand. His thick winter coat provided more than adequate protection against the 23-degree temperature, but for extra protection he had curled his brushy tail across his exposed nose.

Even when sleeping, every one of his senses was tuned to the detection of potential prey—whether the high-pitched squeak of a meadow vole tunneling beneath leaf litter, the faint scent of a deer foraging several hundred yards away, or the rustle of a red squirrel scampering through the canopy of red spruce branches.

Although the drive for food was ever present, another drive was slowly becoming equally important. It was the first week of February when the coywolf picked up a scent more attractive than potential prey. As Adirondus approached a dead balsam fir, the alluring sex attractant of a female coyote in estrus drifted by. His search for food was immediately abandoned. The female was not in the immediate vicinity, but Adirondus followed the scent she had left earlier that night.

Adirondus eagerly trailed the female and was rewarded by further urine signs, reinforcing that she was indeed entering estrus. Throughout the night and most of the next day he pursued, and as darkness approached, he spotted the reddish-brown coyote hunting through a grassy area.

She was less than 40 yards away and searching for meadow voles. He watched curiously, as she cocked her head in one direction and then the other—an attempt to pinpoint the exact location of the rodent. Coming to a halt, she jumped high into the air, arched her back, then descended with stiffened front legs. She plunged her muzzle into the snow and retrieved a struggling vole.

The coywolf cautiously approached and the coyote snarled and dropped onto her belly, while retaining a firm grip on the vole. Adirondus began to circle her, but stopped and sat on his haunches when she bit and swallowed her snack. She jumped to her feet and began a wild dash through the snow. Adirondus began pursuit at a leisurely pace. He was easily able to keep pace with the smaller female.

After a short run, the coyote stopped and crouched in the snow. Adirondus came to within 15 yards and crouched as well. His playful yip seemed to reassure the coyote, and she made no effort to escape.

The female was the only coyote living on the northern end of the Dolly Sods, and their attraction was mutual. The large size of Adirondus was not a deterrent to the coyote, who weighed nearly 40 pounds, and may have even been an attraction.

Courtship became more intimate during the following three weeks, during which time they engaged in play and mutual grooming of face, ears, and back. They slept curled against one another. One day the female, with crouching posture and diverted tail, openly solicited the male. Sexual activity became frequent.

The two solidified their bond as they hunted together the following week. They expanded their hunting territory, searching from one side of the plateau to the other, and jointly marked their territory.

Running adjacent to Dolly Sods on the west was a unique geological feature bearing the name Canaan Valley [pronounced ku-naan]. While Dolly Sods was situated at about 4,000-foot elevation, the broad floor of Canaan Valley lay an abrupt 1,000 feet below.

The climate of Dolly Sods was surprisingly similar to that of southern Canada, but coyote and coywolf suffered little from the cold and near constant howling winds. Hunting activities produced adequate body heat, and daytime was spent curled into a ball beneath the protection of a dense stand of red spruce. With bushy tails covering their faces and a canopy of spruce branches providing stored radiant energy, the pair were relatively comfortable. Heavy snowfalls provided even more protection, as it acted as insulation.

The pair restricted their hunting forays to Dolly Sods throughout February and March. White-tailed deer were abundant for the unusual duo. They found the carcasses of two different deer that had been crippled by human hunters during archery/gun season, and they seldom went more than three days without eating.

Meadow voles were their most dependable food, but they favored rabbits and hares. Dolly Sods supported small populations of cottontail rabbits and snowshoe hares. While rabbits were inclined to seek shelter in underground burrows during severe weather, hares remained above ground in all kinds of weather.

The canine pair learned to coordinate their movements, maintaining a separation of 20 to 30 yards. The scent of a hiding hare prompted an intense search, followed by the hare's frantic burst from cover. Adirondus, with longer legs, was usually the first to reach the hare. However, at times, the hare changed direction, and the more agile female coyote would make the kill.

Spring snowmelt provided an unusual food source. In late March, Adirondus and his mate (hereafter known as "Alghena"), were returning from their nightly hunt when they heard a sound resembling quacking ducks. Adirondus had hunted ducks along beaver ponds in the Adirondacks and knew their vocalizations.

But these calls appeared to come from hundreds of ducks. Stealthily approaching, they spotted a small pool of open water, about 12 feet in diameter, within a stand of hemlock. Edging closer, he saw hundreds of frogs croaking, swimming, splashing, and chasing one another. From four feet away, he pounced and grabbed a slimy frog in his jaws. Adirondus had captured a wood frog.

During February and March, small, temporary pools of melt water (referred to as ephemeral pools) provided breeding sites for these cold-tolerant frogs. With ice often present on the ponds, they breed and lay eggs. Tadpoles, then four-legged froglets emerge before the bodies of water dry up. They are one of the earliest breeding amphibians in Appalachia and play an important role in maintaining a healthy, diversified ecosystem.

After breeding, adults abandon the pools and disperse into the surrounding forest. They are followed a few weeks later by the transformed young froglets. All spend the summer months foraging on the forest floor consuming countless invertebrates.

While mating in the ponds, adult wood frogs provide food for raccoons. Although adult wood frogs were present in the ephemeral ponds for only a couple months, they provided an important food source for Adirondus and Alghena. A wood frog was only three inches long, but the fleshy hind legs added another three inches.

Many ponds in Dolly Sods contained 200 breeding adults. They were light tan in color, with a distinguishing black mask that extended from the eye to the shoulder. Also quite striking was the prominent white line that ran along their upper lip.

The coyote-coywolf pair developed a strategy to capture dozens of the amphibians from each pond. When one jumped to the water's edge to grab a frog, the frogs typically dove to the pond bottom or swam to the opposite side. However, the frenzied breeding urge was so strong that within two to three minutes males were once again actively competing for females.

While Adirondus was eating his first frog, Alghena moved around to the opposite side of the pond where dozens of frogs were congregated. She crawled close to the edge and pounced into the middle of a clump of them. She grabbed three, and carried her catch back a few feet from the pond's edge.

While she ate, Adirondus crawled close to the water's edge on the opposite side. When small concentrations of adult wood frogs resumed mating, he once again pounced. They consumed several dozen frogs each from a pond. When their attacks became too disruptive, the frogs retreated to the bottom of the pond for an extended period of time. When the waiting period between captures became too long, Adirondus and Alghena moved on.

The pair made their first kill of a healthy deer in late March. A late winter snowstorm had engulfed the Dolly Sods. The gusting winds from the west were caused by the plateau's unusually high elevation and north-south orientation. The winds and ice created "flag trees"—so named because they lacked upper branches on the west side. This unique biological phenomenon was most visible with red spruce.

While coursing through a stand of balsam fir and red spruce, the couple jumped a juvenile deer. The doe was days shy of ten months old. Neither fully grown nor at full strength following winter, she had considerable difficulty moving through deep snows. A crust had formed atop the snow cover, sufficient to support a full-grown coyote or a coywolf—but not enough to support a deer. Although the deer had outrun the pair of canids, it floundered in a deep snowdrift, and Adirondus easily closed the distance.

Had the attack occurred in October, when the deer was stronger and the snows were not yet drifted, the doe could have easily escaped. As food became difficult to find, it had lost over 15 pounds and expended considerable energy digging through snow drifts to obtain grasses.

Within five minutes, Adirondus released his grip and began to tear through the tender skin covering the deer's belly. Liver and kidneys were consumed before he turned his attention to the right front shoulder. Meanwhile, Alghena busily ate the rich red meat of a hindquarter.

TUCKER COUNTY COYWOLF PACK

During the first week of April, Alghena discovered an abandoned den of a groundhog (also known as woodchuck). She spent several daytime hours instinctively enlarging the tunnel entrance and den. The 15-foot long tunnel curled around a sunken boulder before culminating at the oval den. When the den was large enough for her to stretch out comfortably, she had a home ready for any future pups that might be born.

This litter would be the first for the two-year old coyote, but she efficiently prepared a den without knowing why. Throughout most of the year, coyotes spend very little time in a den. They curl into a ball beneath a clump of trees, or beside a fallen trunk, protected by a dense fur coat. They seem to prefer an exposed bedding site. Perhaps their senses function more efficiently unhindered by the walls of an underground den.

Adirondus and Alghena hunted together nightly throughout April, returning to the den for the day. One evening, while approaching the carcass of a deer, they discovered a gray fox feeding on the skeleton. Ravens had cleaned much of the flesh from the larger leg bones, but considerable meat remained between the ribs. The gray fox was strong enough to crush the ends of exposed rib bones but could not crush heavier sections or separate major leg bones from the carcass.

The fox's scent reached Adirondus when he and Alghena were nearly

30 yards away, as they approached the carcass from downwind. This tactic allowed them to detect the presence of others, while screening their own scent. Although they did not fear any other predators, even black bears, they did not want to suddenly find themselves face-to-face with one.

Adirondus began a slow, crouching stalk towards the fox and Alghena paralleled him to his left. Seven yards away, Adirondus spotted it against the snow. As if by some silent signal, Adirondus and Alghena simultaneously dropped, crouching even lower in the two-foot deep snow. The fox was too preoccupied to notice them. For most wild animals, the cost of carelessness is death.

Coyotes very much dislike foxes. While there are no scientific data for attributing dislike or hate to a wild animal, it describes the behavior of coyotes towards foxes. A coyote will make every attempt to kill the smaller canine. Foxes and coyotes are certainly competitors. Coyotes and foxes vie for the same prey, especially small rodents and rabbits. As coyote populations have expanded across North America, fox populations have declined.

Adirondus exploded from the snow towards the unsuspecting fox and Alghena was a second behind. The fox darted from the carcass but managed only five frantic leaps before being overpowered by Adirondus. Adirondus and Alghena tore apart the fox, consuming its flesh in large gulps.

In 15 minutes most of the 11-pound fox was devoured. The pair then moved back to the deer carcass and ate for the next two hours. They bedded nearby, then in the morning Alghena led them back to her den. She immediately entered the underground home and snarled menacingly at Adirondus when he attempted to crawl in behind her. He reluctantly accepted the message, and curled up in the snow among the branches of a fallen aspen tree. Alghena had dug the burrow to fit her smaller stature, and not those of the coywolf—thus effectively sealing him out.

The two continued to hunt together until mid-May when Alghena's behavior abruptly changed. Adirondus called to her one evening, inviting her to the nightly hunt. However, she remained in the den. He pushed his long snout into the den opening, and emitted an inviting whine. The female snarled and he reluctantly went on a solitary hunt.

Five squirming pups joined Alghena the following day, and the coywolf population of Dolly Sods increased to six. Although only 25 percent of the pups' DNA could be assigned to timber wolf lineage, the term "coywolf" is appropriate.

The newborn pups were cloaked in dark, tawny, brown fur. Their heads were blunt, their ears were rounded, and the pads of their feet were pink. At ten days of age, their teeth began to push through, and the pads of their feet turned black. By two weeks, their eyes were open. At three weeks, milk incisors erupted through their gums and the pups began to walk around the den. The tips of their floppy ears slowly began to stiffen and their hearing improved significantly.

For the next two weeks, Alghena remained at the den. Following his instincts, Adirondus carried food to Alghena nightly, before satisfying his own hunger. Many nights in May he went without eating, with all captured prey fed to his mate. In early June, five fully-haired, bright-eyed pups began making short trips outside the den entrance.

With the arrival of the pups, Adirondus had been forced to expand his hunting territory and hours. In deep snow, the coywolf had restricted his hunting to the Dolly Sods plateau. Although tempted to explore the jumble of boulders that formed the Allegheny Front, and especially Bear Rocks, he never advanced more than 15 to 20 feet into the formidable maze. On several prior occasions, snow collapsed and he fell into deep, straight-sided crevices—spending hours searching for a means of escape.

When snows melted, and safe passageways were visible, Adirondus again began exploring the mass of boulders. He discovered several routes by which he could safely descend, where he was rewarded with a new food source. Bordering the long line of boulders on the downhill side was an oak forest. Oaks did not grow in Dolly Sods due to severe wintry weather conditions, but on the lower, east-facing slopes of the Potomac River drainage, they were the dominant tree.

Oaks produce acorns, supporting gray squirrels, which were active only during daylight hours. Newborn litters of squirrels were safely secluded in tree cavities, and not accessible to the coywolf. He spent several hours stalking gray squirrels immediately following daybreak, but he became frustrated when they easily escaped by climbing trees.

On his fifth visit to the oak forest, Adirondus discovered a rodent that provided several meals. Along the lower edge of the boulders was a scent that he had not previously encountered. The odor of every animal that lived in the area was quite distinct, and Adirondus changed his hunting strategy to fit behaviors of the specific prey species involved. The strange new scent emanated from within the rock maze itself but was inaccessible to the coywolf.

One night in early May, Adirondus was stalking along the limestone formation when he heard the rustling of leaves. His keen eyesight identified boulders and tree trunks, but no animal. However, scent and sound were all that was needed to pinpoint the location of an animal. Adirondus pounced when the animal moved to within seven feet, and was rewarded with a squirrel-sized rodent.

Adirondus had captured his first woodrat. The woodrat of eastern forests is commonly referred to as the Allegheny woodrat and is rather "attractive" for a rodent. Its soft, gray coat, long whiskers, large bulbous eyes, prominent rounded ears, white feet, white belly, and smooth, hair-covered tail offer a pleasing appearance—to certain humans and probably to most other woodrats. When captured in a trap or surprised at night with a spotlight, it will often sit upright on its haunches, presenting the appearance of someone's pet cat.

Nuts, fruits, and short sections of succulent woody stems are foraged and carried back into a woodrat's home during autumn months, where they are dried and stored in food caches. Thus, during winter months, when snow buries available foods, woodrats enjoy the protection of a relatively warm home and an abundant food supply. Adirondus learned to wait patiently along trails routinely used by woodrats departing their lairs, and captured dozens, each weighing three-quarters of a pound.

To satisfy Alghena's increased needs for food, he expanded his hunting territory even further. The western edge of the Dolly Sods plateau overlooked an oval valley, known as Canaan Valley. This 35,000-acre valley supported the highest-elevation shrub swamp wetland east of the Mississippi River. The southern end contained Canaan Valley State Park and Timberline Ski Resort. The northern end of the Valley was dominated by the 16,000-acre Canaan Valley National Wildlife Refuge. Numerous hiking trails traversed the refuge, but only six miles of dirt road disrupted the unique ecosystem, which resembled segments of Canada.

The Valley floor was ideal hunting conditions. Had it been forested, as it was in the 1800s, habitat would have been marginal for a coyote. One or two packs of timber wolves visited the area in the early 1800s, but they were wiped out by overhunting by 1900. And, with the new century came the loggers.

Following the resulting clear cutting, and subsequent burning of immense amounts of slash, a unique new habitat of shrubs emerged, instead of trees. The Canaan Valley area would never be the same. Never again would herds of elk and buffalo roam freely and never again would packs of timber wolves shatter the quiet of night with their howls. And, never again would the Valley floor be dominated by trees.

The most common of the multiple-stemmed shrubs were alder, blueberry, spiraea, St. John's-wort, viburnum, and shrub willow. Interspersed among the shrub thickets were stands of perennial plants such as bracken fern, flat-topped aster, goldenrod, and various grasses.

The resulting landscape was the most diverse east of the Mississippi River. Usually when extensive clear cutting occurs, a young stand of trees typically grows back. But not in Canaan Valley, or Dolly Sods. A major factor preventing the regrowth of trees was white-tailed deer. White-tailed deer were nearly non-existent during the 1900-1930 period, primarily due to over-hunting. However, with a lack of predators and an abundance of regrowth of vegetation, deer numbers increased steadily. By 1950, the area was overpopulated.

A secondary factor affecting regrowth of trees was temperature. The bowl of the Valley acted as a frost pocket, and cold air commonly rolled down off the surrounding hillsides and settled over the Valley floor. Tender tree seedlings not consumed by hungry deer were often killed by low temperatures. High soil saturation, soil type, and the 3,000-foot elevation all played a role in limiting many tree species.

A complex of wetlands and diverse shrub communities on the Valley floor created optimum hunting for coyotes. Rodents, ranging in size from meadow voles to beaver, could be consistently stalked. However, the one animal that is most essential to coyotes was scarce in Canaan Valley. That was the rabbit.

Although scattered New England cottontail and snowshoe hare existed high on the Dolly Sods plateau, neither existed in the Valley. There were very few blackberry thickets, which are crucial to rabbits for both food and cover. Only in May, when newborn deer were present, did an abundance of easily-obtained food exist in Canaan Valley.

An advantage of the Valley floor was the excellent visibility, often two or three miles. One morning, Adirondus spotted dozens of ravens circling west of Glade Run. After a slow stalk, in which he carefully moved upwind, he saw ravens and turkey vultures cleaning the flesh of a dead beaver. Adirondus scattered the scavengers and took possession of the orange-toothed rodent. Its flesh was still relatively fresh, and provided a nourishing meal. After two hours pulling fatty chunks of flesh from the stiff carcass, Adirondus departed, leaving bones and hide for the birds.

Ravens came to be an unwitting ally, their noisy presence locating numerous carcasses that spring. Although most of his hunting was at night, Adirondus typically chose a daytime resting spot where he could scan a large portion of the sky. The stark silhouettes of ravens, turkey vultures, and crows were easily visible against the sky. And even when asleep, Adirondus was alert to the throaty croaks of ravens.

In early April after most snow had melted, the access road (FR 75) close to the southern end of Bear Rocks was opened. Memorial Day brought a heavy influx of hikers attracted to the 20 or so hiking trails that meander across Dolly Sods plateau, while others traveled FR 75 in pickup trucks and SUV's. The isolation and quietness that had attracted Adirondus to the area no longer existed, that same quality now drawing humans.

Fortunately Alghena's den was over two miles northwest of Bear Rocks. Raven Ridge Trail (TR 521), the nearest hiking trail, was more than one mile to the south. Although some hikers camped along the trails, no campfires were visible from Alghena's den. Alghena likely would have moved her pups to a secondary den had a human approached, but she never felt compelled to.

The most dependable food source for the coywolf was the meadow vole, which lived in abundance beneath dense layers of grass and was one of the first mammals to produce young each spring. Adirondus spent long hours each night hunting quietly through dense grass cover.

A slight shaking of grass stems, a rustle of leaves, or the faint whiff of vole odor was all Adirondus needed. With ears pointed forward, golden yellow eyes focused, and nostrils sucking in the magic scent of food, the location of the vole was determined. Stalking within two feet, the coywolf leapt high into the air, arched his back, then plunged his snout and front paws onto the vole.

Although the largest of all mice in the region, voles were easily swallowed whole. At times, he captured two or three before carrying them in his mouth back to Alghena. Meadow voles intended for the pups were eaten, then regurgitated at the den. At four weeks old, the pups began eating this warm, softened, stew-like meat.

Larger mammals, like groundhogs, cottontail rabbits, and snowshoe hare produced young in April and May, but were not reliably available for Adirondus. Young groundhogs and cottontails remained underground until nearly half grown, while young snowshoe hares remained immobile within shallow depressions, so none were significant prey for the coywolf.

White-tailed deer began dropping their fawns in May, and Adirondus slowly shifted his focus to this easy prey. A single fawn was under ten pounds, and could be carried intact back to Alghena. Does typically had their newborn in dense grassy areas, out of sight from aerial and ground predators. The newborns gave off only a faint scent. By remaining motionless when their mother was away, most managed to stay safe.

Predators develop a "search image" for specific types of prey, as seasons change. For example, predators utilized scent in specific habitats, but visually spotted them in other instances. To locate newborn fawns, Adirondus developed a strategy of moving slowly through every thick patch of grasses or ferns or goldenrod he encountered. He focused his efforts on the faint cues: a fawn's unique scent, the nervous flicking of its ears, or even the buzzing of deer flies attracted to its head.

Young fawns are a bright, reddish-brown color, with numerous white spots serving to break the animal's outline. However, Adirondus never searched for reddish-brown patches in the grasses as he was almost completely colorblind. Reds appeared gray to Adirondus. All members of the Canidae family are colorblind, as are most other mammals. Black bears are an exception. They have the ability to see most colors, although reds appear subdued to them.

Orange and green appear yellow to coyotes, but can be distinguished from red. These carnivores are capable of differentiating between violet, yellow, orange, and red, based on how bright or dark they appear. Blue and yellow are the only colors that appear realistic to a coyote.

When fawns reached two weeks old, they no longer remained motionless when their mother was away. Fawns younger than three weeks old were not fast enough to escape a coyote or coywolf. Although they would not play a role in expanding the white-tailed deer population, their death contributed to the survival of the first litter of coywolf pups to appear on Dolly Sods.

When a prey animal realizes it has been discovered and attack by a predator is imminent, it has three options: freeze, flee, or fight. A newborn fawn knows instinctively to freeze, but when one to two weeks old, it is likely to choose the flight option.

In June, when the gaudy blooms of mountain laurel and flame azalea brought the first seasonal burst of color to the plateau, a smorgasbord of foods became available. Not coincidentally, this was when the demands of Alghena and the five pups were greatest.

In May and June, the northern end of Canaan Valley produced a greater variety of foods than Dolly Sods. More than 120 beaver ponds dotted the Valley—the engineering works of several dozen beaver. Although nearly half the ponds were deserted, they still supported water snakes, meadow voles, and careless young muskrats which Adirondus captured.

A seasonal treat in May and June was eggs. Adirondus discovered nests of red-winged blackbirds in the dense marsh around beaver ponds, and by rearing on his hind legs he managed to dump eggs (or nestlings) onto the ground. He also discovered several large female snapping turtles in search of a suitable location to deposit their tough-shelled eggs. The jaws of an adult snapping turtle were so dangerous that Adirondus avoided them.

However, the discovery of a clutch of eggs was a different story. After laying as many as 30 eggs in a hole she had dug, the snapper covered the eggs and returned to the beaver pond. The odor of eggs and freshly exposed damp soil provided all the evidence Adirondus needed to initiate digging. Usually buried only six to eight inches deep, the round, white, ping-pong ball-sized eggs were pulled out and eaten one by one.

The snapping turtle was never aware that her egg laying efforts had been for naught, and she would make no other nesting attempts that spring. In contrast, female wild turkey, red-winged blackbirds, and mallard ducks would all renest that same spring if their first clutch of eggs was destroyed.

Adirondus was not the only animal searching for eggs. One June night, as a light rain fell over the Valley, he noted the scent of another foraging mammal. The coywolf was hunting on elevated areas of barren soil near the Blackwater River, where a logging railroad had once operated. The mixture of cinders and gravel was ideal for a nesting snapping turtle.

Adirondus had discovered two turtle nests in the area the previous week and was searching for newly-disturbed soil. The southerly breeze brought the sounds of nearby digging, and the coywolf circled to be downwind of the source. He soon recognized the scent of a raccoon, who was even better equipped to excavate a turtle nest. The raccoon had one advantage—"hands" capable of reaching into a hole and grasping an egg.

The male raccoon was in the process of pulling out his third egg, when Adirondus leapt through the air and landed atop him. Adirondus broke the raccoon's back, and began tearing apart the black-masked competitor even before its death throes had ended. At nearly 30 pounds, the raccoon provided enough meat for Adirondus to fill his stomach, after which he dug out the last four turtle eggs to complete his meal. With his stomach full, he returned to the den and regurgitated a unique blend of eggs and raccoon meat for the pups.

A second source of eggs provided even more nourishment. In the pre-dawn hours, while hunting, a powerful scent emanated from the brush pile created by a fallen birch tree. A windstorm had uprooted the tree the previous winter, and a hen turkey had selected a small opening to build her nest. She actually just scratched enough to create a cleared spot and began laying eggs in the depression. One brown-flecked egg was deposited each day, until 14 eggs were present.

If nothing disturbed the eggs, 28 days after the last egg was laid they would hatch, and the turkey poults would follow their mother around, consuming whatever insects and invertebrates they could capture. The hen would take her poults to prime foraging habitats, but she would never directly feed them. Similar to other precocial species, including snapping turtles, wood frogs, water snakes, ducks, and geese, turkey poults must get their own food to survive.

The wild turkey scent was all the evidence Adirondus needed. In less than two minutes, he encroached so close to the hen that she frantically flushed from the eggs. Instinctively, Adirondus lunged, but was only rewarded with tail feathers. He had no chance of catching her as she flew off so he returned to the fallen treetop. Soon he was enjoying breakfast of turkey eggs. Each egg was carefully grasped in his jaws before cracking the shell. Yellow yolks were swallowed and any drippings were licked up.

OTHER PREDATORS

One night Adirondus heard the squeal of an injured rabbit. There are few sounds as appealing to a coyote as a rabbit crying in pain. Adirondus immediately circled to put himself downwind. Just 15 yards from the squealing rabbit, he dropped low to the ground and began a crouching stalk. At five yards, he picked up rabbit scent—as well as that of a bobcat.

Bobcats are efficient predators of rabbits; and nine adult bobcats were full-time residents of the Dolly Sods plateau. Most male bobcats tip the scales at 30 pounds, less than half the 70-pound coywolf. Adirondus half-heartedly chased every bobcat he encountered, but all easily escaped by climbing trees.

The rabbit had been ambushed by a female bobcat. The feline sat patiently along a well-used rabbit trail for nearly two hours before seeing the hapless rabbit.

The thick fur of the cat was tannish brown and dotted with scattered spots. Her most distinguishing characteristic was a short five-inch tail. The cat had a litter of four kittens, asleep in a den deep within the boulders of Bear Rocks. Unlike coyotes, a male bobcat does not assist its mate when she is nursing young. The female bobcat spent daylight hours in the den with her young, but left every night to hunt.

With no warning, Adirondus struck the bobcat on her left hip. She snarled in surprise, dropped the rabbit, and bolted through the alder thicket. The coywolf made no attempt to pursue, finding the struggling rabbit, and 30 minutes later dropped the limp rabbit on the bare dirt of his den's entrance. His low-pitched whine informed Alghena that food was available. She rewarded him with a lick on the face, and then tore into the rabbit flesh. Needing food himself, Adirondus resumed his hunt, but was unsuccessful.

Opportunistic Adirondus ate both vertebrates and invertebrates. In June, large numbers of grasshoppers were present in the goldenrod and bracken fern stands. These two-inch-long insects were favored by many birds, including turkey poults.

While following a family of turkeys through a grassy field, Adirondus became distracted by hundreds of jumping grasshoppers. He soon developed an effective search image, spotting a resting grasshopper on a grass stem. If the light green insects jumped a short distance and landed within sight, Adirondus would stalk close enough to make a capture. But if the grasshopper flew, often for five to ten feet, he would lose sight of it. An hour spent hunting grasshoppers produced more pounds of food than did a search for turkey poults. Adirondus consumed over five dozen grasshoppers that morning before returning to the den.

On Dolly Sods, only one predator was larger than the coywolf— the black bear. An adult female weighed at least 250 pounds, while males weighed slightly more. Black bears were omnivores, consuming more plant matter than animal matter during summer and fall months. However, during May and June bears were competing for the same newborn deer fawns. Black bears rarely killed a healthy adult deer, but readily fed on crippled deer left by hunters.

One evening in June, Adirondus was meandering through a stand of aspen in Canaan Valley. He turned his attention to the bracken fern, goldenrod, and St. John's-wort which formed the understory beneath the aspen stand. He had captured a fawn in that same patch of aspen in May. Unbeknownst to Adirondus, a black bear sow and her two cubs were searching the same aspen stand.

The female had given birth in February to the two cubs in a deep den she had dug beneath the root mass of a fallen red spruce. The cubs nursed several times each day, while their mother remained in a hibernation stupor. At three months of age, the female and her energetic cubs departed the den.

The cubs weighed less than a pound at birth, but by May, when they left their den, they weighed five pounds. They continued to nurse several times every day, then rested while their mother was consuming large quantities of tender, newly emerged grasses, skunk cabbage, ants, and ant eggs. Having lost one-third of her weight during hibernation, she was driven to regain weight and provide milk to her insatiable cubs.

While the black bear wandered through the understory, her cubs explored the myriad odors in the aspen stand. One cub had wandered 15 yards away when Adirondus spotted it. Thinking it was a fawn, he leapt on its back and clamped his jaws onto its shoulder. The loose skin on the cub's back prevented it being a fatal bite. The cub squalled in pain as mother rushed to its aid, letting out a ferocious roar, causing Adirondus to release his grip. The cub ran to the closest tree and scrambled up to the lowest limb.

The second cub shadowed its mother, curious to discover what was causing the commotion. Adirondus spotted its black form and rushed in its direction. Again, the mother bear let out a loud roar, and that caused the second cub to climb another aspen tree. Adirondus stood on his hind legs and again was frustrated by a cub being out of reach. The bear then rushed the coywolf, who returned to the tree holding the first cub. For nearly 20 minutes, the bear continued rushing towards the agile coywolf, who alternated between the two trees and cubs.

Had Alghena been with Adirondus, the two might have distracted the mother bear with continuous attacks, prompting one of the cubs to descend from the tree. But, the coywolf was not powerful enough to drive off the bear, and reluctantly left. Adirondus would meet the bears numerous times that summer, but as the cubs grew he ceased all efforts to capture one.

Adirondus encountered another mammal one morning in May. These mid-sized squirrels, also known as "fairy diddles," are slightly smaller than gray squirrels, and similar in size to woodrats. Red squirrels feed almost exclusively on seeds of red spruce. They also create food caches and store thousands of seeds underground or in hollow stumps.

The coywolf was focused on a scolding red squirrel sitting on a limb about 12 feet off the ground. The flicking tail and ratchet-like call made the reddish rodent obvious as Adirondus crouched low to the ground, eager to pursue if it foolishly returned to the ground.

A fisher, the largest weasel in the Valley suddenly appeared. The fisher was dark brown and had a bushy tail similar to a mink. A male fisher has a total length (tail included) of 35 to 40 inches, while the male mink has a length of only 19 to 29 inches. Fishers prefer upland forest and mink prefer lowland aquatic habitats.

The fisher trotting through the spruce stand that morning was carrying a red squirrel. Her den in a hollow log held four hungry pups. The coywolf spied the fisher, and forgot the scolding red squirrel. When the fisher was within 15 yards, Adirondus erupted. He was within five yards when the fisher heard him. Adirondus would have easily killed any other mid-sized predator, but the fisher had an advantage of being an excellent tree climber.

Fishers, once called the "black fox," were common throughout the Central Appalachians in the 1700s and early 1800s. By 1900, trapping and logging had eliminated this furbearer from West Virginia.

In an effort to restore wildlife species that had been historically abundant, the West Virginia Division of Natural Resources (WVDNR) initiated a program in the 1960s to reintroduce several extirpated species. In 1969, 23 fishers were obtained from New Hampshire in exchange for West Virginia wild turkeys. Fifteen fishers were released on Canaan

Mountain and at Canaan Heights, in Tucker County. The other eight were released in Pocahontas County.

The reintroduction of the fisher was one of the most successful releases ever undertaken by the WVDNR. In 10 years, fishers had expanded their range to Grant and Preston counties. By 2015, fishers were in 23 of the 55 West Virginia counties.

Snowshoe hare, rabbits, squirrels, chipmunks, mice, voles, shrews, and moles are frequently consumed by these agile predators. The diets of fishers and coyotes/coywolves were somewhat similar, and the two frequently competed for the same food. The coyote was an omnivore, while the fisher was strictly a carnivore.

The most unique aspect of fisher feeding behavior involves porcupines, the largest animal commonly killed by fishers. Fishers kill and consume more porcupines than any other species. No other mammal actively searches for and attacks porcupines. Only the belly and face of porcupines are not protected by quills. Fishers sometimes flip a porcupine onto its back to kill it but more often they attack its face. Repeated bites to the face, often over a period of 30 minutes, frequently kill this large, bark-chewing rodent.

Although porcupines can climb trees, so can fishers. A fisher has hind feet that can rotate nearly 180 degrees, enabling it to descend a tree headfirst. Fishers exhibit a greater degree of arborality (tree-climbing skills) than any other large mammals. Porcupines in the Dolly Sods/ Canaan Valley area are scarce, so they are not significant to fisher diets.

Adirondus was within three feet when the frightened fisher dropped the squirrel and scampered up a red spruce. She stopped on the first large branch and stared down. The two exchanged glares for several minutes, then Adirondus picked up the dead squirrel and headed to his ever-hungry mate.

Several avian predators also competed with Adirondus and Alghena for food. Barred owls and red-tailed hawks sought rabbits, while goshawks, kestrels (sparrow hawks), saw-whet owls, and broad-winged hawks captured and consumed hundreds of small birds and rodents. Golden eagles, present mainly in winter, consumed larger prey, such as white-tailed deer.

A healthy ecosystem must contain a balanced number of plants, herbivores, and carnivores. Where there is life, there must also be death. In a stable population, the number born equals the number dying. If more die in any one year, the population decreases. If fewer die, the population increases. Such increases cannot continue indefinitely, or the ecosystem will suffer.

The future of coywolves in Canaan Valley/Dolly Sods was dependent on adequate food to sustain Alghena's litter. Unfortunately, the area did not support an abundance of prey animals, and Adirondus was constantly forced to expand the size of his hunting territory.

EVER-HUNGRY PUPS

At four weeks of age, the coywolf pups engaged in playful combat and serious competition to determine the dominant member. Alghena spent less and less time inside the den with the pups. Fleas were a nuisance, and so were the pups. Weaning the pups was accomplished simply by leaving them, and accompanying her mate on nightly hunts.

The pups weighed three pounds each, and retained many characteristics of a newborn. Their feet and head were still disproportionately large, but their snouts had begun to lengthen. Teeth were present, their ears now stood erect, and most of the litter were tawny brown in color, with one of the females dark gray.

The adults rekindled their cooperative hunting strategies and captures increased significantly. Alghena had lost several pounds while nursing and she needed a kill every day. One morning, after an unsuccessful night of hunting, Alghena spotted a groundhog feeding 40 yards away, and whined a warning to her mate. Groundhogs seldom venture far from their den, and are difficult targets for a single predator.

Alghena began a slow stalk, so low to the ground that her silhouette was hidden from the groundhog. She began a circle around the prey. At the same time, Adirondus started a circle in the opposite direction. When they were on opposite sides of the groundhog, they moved in. The groundhog caught sight of Adirondus when he was 12 yards away, and made a dash for its den—towards Alghena. Just in front of the den entrance, she caught the groundhog, gave two violent shakes, and began her meal. Adirondus sat and watched his mate eat over half of the eight-pound rodent. Only when she ceased eating and stepped away did he step up.

In June, Adirondus and Alghena showed their teamwork again. Mountain laurel bushes were blooming, when they discovered a small flock of Canada geese grazing along a beaver pond. Adirondus had captured only one goose during the months he was providing for Alghena. They always either flew away or swam out into deep water.

Many goose nests are constructed atop beaver lodges in the middle of a pond. Rarely does a predator manage to kill the female goose or eat any of the eggs from such nests. Male geese can drive off mid-sized predators (such as foxes or bobcats), especially when they are swimming to reach a nest.

While searching the shoreline for muskrats, Adirondus discovered a goose sitting on a nest of eggs at the end of a small peninsula jutting into the pond. While working his way onto the narrow peninsula, he was attacked by the gander, whose powerful wings rained harsh blows on his head. The surprised coywolf was knocked into the pond, where he continued to receive blows from the gander's wings. He abandoned the idea of killing a goose that night.

The geese were flightless. Unlike most birds, waterfowl shed the major flight feathers of their wings every June. They regrow new feathers during July, but for about one month they cannot fly. Waterfowl are able to survive this month because they remain along the edge of large bodies of water. When disturbed they simply slip into the water and swim to safety.

During this period, they feed on succulent aquatic vegetation. Because they are so vulnerable, they seldom venture more than 15 yards from the water's edge. Alghena was familiar with this and knew it would be fruitless to stalk the geese.

Alghena made no effort to hide from the geese as she walked to a small knoll 40 yards from the birds. There she sat on her haunches and began waving her tail from side to side. She let out two yips to be certain the geese focused attention on her.

Adirondus was stalking through the head-high vegetation. When he halted his advance, Alghena again moved so that the geese looked towards her. Behind them, Adirondus kept approaching. Alghena continued her conspicuous performance, and the geese kept watching her unusual actions. Two of the geese became nervous and entered the water, but the others remained ashore.

Adirondus was within 12 yards of the geese before he launched his attack. He leapt before they could swim away and bit onto the wing of a goose. Within seconds, the soaked coywolf carried the thrashing, honking prize ashore. Alghena came running and they devoured dark goose flesh, then returned to their den to regurgitate small clumps of meat for their pups.

In July, Alghena moved the pups to an alternate den site. Such moves were common, and meant fewer fleas, and added security due to less coyote scent. She chose a site along the western edge of the Dolly Sods plateau in a small stand of red spruce. The pups were forced to remain at their new den site when their parents were away hunting. Although they tried to follow, warning growls from the adults caused them to turn around.

The pups now weighed ten pounds each, except for a 12-pound female. Her coat was darker than that of her reddish-brown siblings, so that she appeared larger than she actually was. Her feet were also larger. Nearly the same size as her mother's, they were over three inches wide. Her ears were rounded rather than pointed, and her snout was broad rather than narrow and pointed. In each of these ways, she exhibited her more dominant wolf traits.

This female coywolf, hereafter known as "Applacha," was the favorite of Adirondus. During daytime, when the pack slept, Applacha focused most of her attention on her father. She pulled his tail, clamped her jaws around his leg, and napped in direct contact with him. He enjoyed her presence and frequently licked her face and pulled her ears. None of the other pups seemed to desire that attention. Two other young females focused their attention on their mother, while two male pups spent almost all their time together.

In July, Adirondus discovered a major new food source—blueberries. Primarily carnivorous, coyotes/coywolves also consumed plants, especially berries and fruits. Dolly Sods was an optimal site for blueberries and huckleberries. The area had been covered with dense stands of red spruce in the early 1900s, but extensive clearcutting and subsequent wild fires produced soil conditions suitable for blueberries. Hundreds of acres of blueberry thickets provided food for birds, mammals, and humans.

Every year after the summer solstice, hundreds of humans ventured onto Dolly Sods to fill buckets with blueberries. A coyote or coywolf could consume thousands of berries in one night. A single acre of blueberries could satiate the hunger of a coyote, at least for a day. Adirondus and Alghena returned to the same expanse of blueberries for five nights. They only left due to humans coming for the blueberries.

Weekends brought hikers, campers, and barking dogs. The area soon reeked of human scent. Returning to their pups late one night, Adirondus and Alghena passed within 70 yards of the tents of sleeping campers. There were enough human odors and sounds to persuade Adirondus to leave the area.

In mid-July, Adirondus and Alghena called their litter to join them on the nightly hunt. Reluctantly, the pups joined in. Applacha followed closely in her father's footsteps, while her siblings struggled to keep up. Adirondus surprised and captured a young snowshoe hare and allowed his pups to pull the hare apart, each obtaining a mouthful of warm meat.

Soon after, they failed to bring down a young buck along the rim of Cabin Mountain before descending the hill to the Glade Run wetlands. These wetlands were a key component of the Canaan Valley National Wildlife Refuge, lending significant water flow and aquatic habitats. There the adults captured two young muskrats, a juvenile beaver, and numerous meadow voles. Most were already dead when offered to the pups, but a few were still capable of running or jumping, and provided excellent lessons for the pups.

Applacha claimed more than her share of prey and grew more proficient at obtaining her own food. Her first capture was a half-grown meadow vole, and soon she was regularly capturing them. When Adirondus approached the youngsters with a half-grown mallard duck in his jaws, he offered it to Applacha. His dominant offspring successfully defended the prize from her siblings, and she ate the entire duckling.

For the next few weeks, the pups learned to mimic their parents and early evening found them scattered in blueberry thickets, scarfing up mouthfuls of juicy berries. Adirondus and Alghena taught the pups how to harvest the crop efficiently. Sitting on their haunches, they closed their mouths around branches, then "picked" the berries by grasping berries and leaves with their incisors and lips. They made no effort to separate berries from leaves, swallowing both.

Coyotes and coywolves have powerful jaw muscles, and long dagger-like teeth. Sharp-edged premolars enable them to shear off large chunks of flesh, while the broad surfaces of rear molars enable them to crush and grind bones or apples, blueberries and black cherries. Coyotes, foxes, and wolves have in total 42 teeth: 12 incisors, 4 canines, 16 premolars, and 10 molars.

Now independent of a den site, the pack moved nomadically throughout the northern end of Canaan Valley, searching wetlands, hardwood hillsides, and the grassland ecotones that occurred extensively between woodland and wetlands. Adirondus led them along Glade Run, the Little Blackwater, and the main branch of the Blackwater River—covering the entire area between Brown Mountain and Cabin Mountain.

APPLES AND FLYING SQUIRRELS

September brought a drastic increase in humans to the Valley. Hunting was permitted in Canaan Valley National Wildlife Refuge, and Canada goose hunters appeared the first week of September. Adirondus and his pack were moving through an alder thicket, when the shotgun blasts started.

Hunters had hidden themselves in dense cattails and rice cutgrass before daylight. A dense layer of fog limited the visibility of both hunters and geese. As the fog began to burn off, a small flight of geese were attracted to the eight goose decoys the hunters had set out. Three 12-gauge shotguns fired, and two geese fell.

Adirondus and the pack were only 300 yards from the hunters, but it sounded much closer. None of the pups had ever heard a shotgun and panicked. They ran a hundred yards before Adirondus and Alghena caught up with them. Adirondus issued a warning and led the pups another half mile before stopping. He and Alghena comforted their litter by licking their faces.

The next day, Adirondus led them to the sweet scent of apples. Although not yet ripe, three of the insect-scarred fruits had fallen to the ground. Adirondus began gnawing at one apple, and was soon joined by Alghena. She was eating one when the pups arrived.

Only a few dozen scattered apple trees were in Canaan Valley. Most were over 100 years old and probably came from cores discarded by loggers and railroaders, or plantings of early settlers and farmers.

In the mid-1800s, Canaan Valley was covered with red spruce, eastern hemlock, and black cherry. Because of the abundant timber and coal, in 1885 Henry Gassaway Davis established the town that bears his name and built the West Virginia Central & Pittsburg Railway. A sawmill was constructed in Davis in 1886 and a tannery (for cattle hides) was constructed shortly after. A few years later, a pulp mill was added.

Between 1887 and 1890, several splash dams were built across the Blackwater River to accommodate floating the logs to the mill. However, problems with timing and the flow of water from the dams created major logistical problems. Consequently, small-gauge logging railroads were constructed into all major stands of timber. Logging in the 1890s cleared huge areas of Canaan Valley, and the once glorious forest was changed forever.

By 1920, logging had ceased and numerous catastrophic forest fires followed. Many were caused by sparks from the railroad, while others resulted from lightning as logging debris dried. By the 1940s, lands had been cleared, crops were being grown, and livestock wandered freely through the widespread grasslands. Ultimately, a greater diversity of habitat emerged in Canaan Valley than in any other portion of the Central Appalachian Mountains.

After eating the few apples, Adirondus led his pack southward. Around midnight, Alghena picked up the scent of deer and quietly signaled the pack. They closed in behind her, and all six canines eased quietly through the head-high vegetation. Four does and two half-grown fawns sprang from the stand of alder where they had been bedding.

The key to a successful coywolf/coyote hunt was stamina. They weren't able to run down a deer quickly. A chase typically covered several hundred yards, or even half a mile. Upon discovering a deer, they started chasing to try to find any weakness. Adirondus and Alghena were capable of identifying an unusual gait, an inconsistent run, an awkward posture, and a multitude of other behaviors unique to handicapped individuals.

They couldn't waste energy pursuing healthy deer, or risk injury attacking one.

After a 400-yard chase, a yearling attempted to cross Sand Run. Unfortunately, she had injured her left shoulder in a snowdrift the previous February. As a result, the landscape belied her weakness. The stream was only two feet deep and 12 feet wide, but the deer became entangled attempting to surmount two large boulders. One foot got wedged as she struggled to free herself. Applacha sprang from the bank and chomped down onto the deer's left hindquarter. Adirondus joined her, and in less than five minutes, father and daughter had dragged the deer out of the stream.

The whole family voraciously ate for an hour. They slept most of the night then returned to the carcass at daybreak. They ate much of the remaining 65-pound carcass, then abandoned the hide, bones, and other scattered remains. By late afternoon, a dozen turkey vultures had descended to clean up the carcass. A gray fox also visited, but had to break the ends off rib bones and gnaw out the marrow to gain any nourishment.

The pack continued moving south, while working up the Sand Run watershed. The next night they passed the southern boundary of Canaan Valley National Wildlife Refuge and heard roaring water. They reached an earthen, man-made dam built in the early 1980s to provide recreation for people at Timberline. That 2,700-acre development contained 451 houses, 46 owned by permanent homeowners and 405 by vacation homeowners. In addition, it contained two lakes, Sand Run and Spruce Island.

Adirondus picked up strong human scent as he led the pack along the crest of a dam. Following construction of the dam, four houses were built within 200 yards. The pack rested in the darkness atop the dam. Sounds of humans emanated from two houses, and the barking of a dog from another. Scents and sounds of humans were too much for Adirondus, and he led his pack back onto the Refuge.

One night in September, Adirondus was leading his pack trying to surprise a deer. He picked up the odor of a rodent and dropped to his belly and whined an "alert" signal to the others. All knew food was present, even if they did not know what kind.

Because their eyes contained an abundance of rods (specialized cells for seeing in low light) they could see objects at night we can't see. They were capable of seeing only in black and white at night, similar to what humans might experience as darkness settles over the landscape. Most of their potential prey had night vision capabilities, and the predators were often detected before their prey.

With a slight breeze blowing into his face, Adirondus eased forward. He heard rustling and estimated its size based on the amount of scent. Instinctively he concluded it was the size of a chipmunk or small red squirrel. He continued to inch forward, and launched himself. The prey detected the approaching shadow along with coywolf odor, and scampered towards the nearest tree trunk. It reached the trunk and started climbing upwards. However, before it reached the first low limb, Adirondus leapt upwards and clamped his jaws onto the small animal.

It was a West Virginia northern flying squirrel. The head and body portion of this male was six inches long, with a five-inch tail. At six ounces, it was only a snack. He quickly swallowed, sharing none with his mate or his young. The hungry pack hunted for several hours and managed to locate one other northern flying squirrel, but it escaped to a spruce tree and entered a wooden nest box.

The nest box of cedar was one of 30 that had been erected along the upper reaches of the ski resort. This animal was officially listed as endangered by the U.S. Fish and Wildlife Service (USFWS) in July 1985. Its population was thought to be jeopardized by habitat loss, human disturbance, and competition with the more common southern flying squirrel. The federal listing also warned that the quantity and quality of red spruce forests were in jeopardy.

Prior to 1985, only ten West Virginia northern flying squirrels had been documented. All ten were captured in West Virginia between elevations of 3,300 feet and 4,400 feet. Flying squirrels are nocturnal, and few persons enter red spruce forests at night, and even fewer view one. And, it is nearly impossible to distinguish between a southern flying squirrel and a northern flying squirrel.

Following the USFWS listing in 1985, wildlife biologists from the WVDNR, Monongahela National Forest (MNF), and West Virginia University (WVU) initiated surveys to determine the distribution and habitat preferences of the northern flying squirrel. The two basic techniques used were live trapping and nest boxes. The 30 nest boxes at Timberline Ski Resort were part of the more than 600 boxes distributed.

Nest boxes were examined two or three times a year. A biologist would climb a ladder, stuff an old wool sock into the small entrance hole, then carry the box to the ground. He would slide open the front door and examine the box for nest material or living occupants. Wire screen prevented any creatures from escaping. If flying squirrels were present they were identified, weighed, sexed, and labeled with a small aluminum, numbered ear tag. Captures in nest boxes and live traps from 1985-2015 totaled nearly 1,600 squirrels, 260 of which were in Tucker County.

In March 2013, the USFWS issued a ruling, removing the West Virginia northern flying squirrel from the federal list of endangered and threatened wildlife. Data indicated the numbers of northern flying squirrels were stable—and the acreage of red spruce forest was increasing. Because as much as 70 percent of habitat is located within the Monongahela National Forest, a favorable forecast of this high-elevation species exists.

These squirrels glide rather than fly and feed primarily on underground mushrooms (fungi), which are not visible to humans— or coywolves. These hypogeous (underground) species of mushrooms apparently have a distinctive odor to the squirrels. Adirondus and his pack searched red spruce forests on several nights during September, but didn't encounter another foraging flying squirrel.

YELLOW IS SEPTEMBER

Yellow was the color of September, while reds dominated in October. Goldenrod filled many of the fields, and with its tint the entire ground assumed a yellowish-tan hue. Ferns and grasses likewise were turning yellow, while birch and beech, and a few red maple, contributed to the yellow show. And in a final change, the brilliant golden glow of aspens would appear in October.

It was the leaves of black cherry that were first among the trees to provide a hint of what was to come. By the middle of August, numerous yellow leaves of black cherry trees were silently floating earthward. But none of these color changes were noticed by the color blind pack. Of greater interest to Adirondus was the maturing of black cherry fruits. Those raisin-sized fruits provided many pounds of nourishment for his pack. Maturing at the same time were the similar-sized fruits of viburnums.

Blue jays and other songbirds fluttered through the canopies of black cherry stands, harvesting the fruits before they were fully ripened. They competed with ruffed grouse, wild turkey, chipmunks, raccoons, and black bear—all capable of accessing the highest branches of the trees.

One night, as a quarter moon was beginning to descend, Adirondus heard splashing at an abandoned beaver pond. Even at six feet away, he could neither see nor smell the prey. The coywolf cautiously took two more steps before pouncing. Expecting to meet warm, soft fur or feathers, he was surprised when his jaws closed around a cold, smooth, somewhat solid object that began thrashing wildly. It emitted no squeaks or squawks, but flailed violently and smacked Adirondus' face. And most shocking, it sank a mouthful of needle-sharp teeth into his lip.

He had pounced on a large snake. It was over three feet long, and provided such a tussle that Adirondus struggled to maintain his grip. The snake repeatedly bit him on the face, but Adirondus would not let go. After the snake's backbone was severed, it continued thrashing for several more minutes. Adirondus' sharp premolars sliced cleanly through the snake, and he began feeding on the front half. Alghena, next upon the scene, claimed the rear half. The youngsters approached, but they were warned back by their parents' snarls since the snake only weighed a pound.

Blood seeped from the pack leader's lips as he swallowed snake meat, though he was unaware it was his own blood. The wounds oozed for 20 minutes, and stung slightly due in part to a mild anticoagulant from the snake's salivary glands. Accustomed to scratches from thorns, Adirondus ignored the stinging pains and resumed his hunt.

Snakes were rare on Dolly Sods and Canaan Valley, and Adirondus had limited experience with them. Humans driving the dirt road atop the Dolly Sods plateau occasionally sighted a timber rattlesnake. These venomous reptiles foraged mainly through the rocky outcroppings along the Allegheny Front, and spent most summers in the oak forest below feeding on chipmunks and squirrels.

No venomous snakes lived here due primarily to cold air and soil— conditions unsuitable for most reptiles. Small snakes, such as the ring-necked, redbelly, garter, and green were scattered in the area, however. The snake that bit Adirondus was dark gray, with dark blotches. Some called it a "moccasin" when they encountered one along streams or beaver ponds.

Adirondus suffered no lasting effects from the snake bites.

Although sharing many features with the venomous water moccasin of southeastern states, the water snake lacked the wedge-shaped head, vertical black pupils, and prominent heat-sensitive facial pits characteristic of the fabled moccasin, rattlesnake, and copperhead. Northern water snakes were the largest species in the area—with the exception of a rare timber rattler on Dolly Sods.

Red maples were one of the most variable of all trees, with October foliage becoming a blend of yellow, orange, and red. This attracted thousands of tourists in October. A few camped overnight, but the majority spent their nights in motels and lodges. Thus, the coywolves were confronted with few sounds of humans during their nighttime hunts.

Members of Alghena's litter were no longer pups. They weighed 25 pounds, with Applacha weighing over 30. The appearance of the large female coywolf closely resembled Adirondus. Her skull resembled that of a wolf, and her legs were longer and more powerful than those of her siblings. Also, her coat was nearly as dark as Adirondus.

The growing youngsters required the pack to hunt 12 to 14 hours every night. Fortunately bow season for deer had opened the first week of October. Although this brought many humans, it also brought an increase in food. Every successful bowhunter left a "gut pile" before dragging out the deer carcass.

After locating the deer, hunters cut open the belly, separated the large stomach paunch and the mass of intestines, and pulled it out. While inedible to most humans, to a coyote or coywolf it provided a feast. Stomach and intestinal contents were ignored by most carnivores, although layers of leaf fat coating the stomach and intestines were readily consumed. Hunger also drove animals to consume the walls of the stomach and the intestine.

Many hunters removed the kidneys, liver, heart, and lungs at the same time as the stomach and intestines. Those organs, with the exception of the lungs, were considered delicacies by some hunters, but others did not want to mess with them and left them behind. In that case, carnivores enjoyed extra special treats.

While trotting along a small tributary of Red Creek, Alghena flushed a fully-grown doe that was bedded within a patch of rhododendron. She yipped to the pack and began chasing. An aluminum arrow protruding from her shoulder had splintered her shoulder blade, severely limiting her running ability. The chase had covered only 300 yards when Alghena and a pup knocked the doe off her feet.

Within minutes, all members of the pack were congregated around the doe awaiting their turn to eat. Adirondus and Alghena as always fed first. Applacha, however, was frequently permitted to feed alongside her parents, but pack hierarchy prevented the other pups from joining. At times, those pups waited anxiously for 30 minutes.

Several days later, Applacha and one of her brothers discovered another wounded doe. They were able to consume prized internal organs before their parents and littermates arrived.

Another evening in late October, Adirondus picked up the faint scent of blood. He yipped to the pack, and they began following the blood trail left by a wounded buck. A bow hunter in a tree stand had taken a shot at the eight-point buck about 25 yards away. Unfortunately, the arrow struck a little too far to the rear and hit the hipbone, a consequence of the bowstring's sound spooking the deer. The five-year old buck was strong enough to run 250 yards before slowing to a limping walk.

The hunter waited 30 minutes in his tree stand, to give the deer time to bed down before he climbed down and attempted to find the blood trail. Darkness forced him to rely on a small flashlight, but after an hour of fruitless searching, he abandoned the search.

The buck died six hours later only 600 yards from the hunter's deer stand. Although his body had stiffened, the meat was still fresh when

Adirondus discovered it around midnight. Briefly hesitating, he then began consuming the hindquarter.

Had the weather been warmer and Adirondus not found the carcass for several days, the pack might not have eaten the deer. They were scavengers, not hesitating to eat dead animals—but only before maggots were present. The buck, a robust and healthy specimen, weighed over 200 pounds and provided several meals for the pack.

Heavy rains began the last week of October, due to a hurricane that struck the Carolinas earlier in the week. There was little wind, but for two days the downpours continued. The pack was searching the hillside above Red Creek, when the smallest female discovered the scent of a deer. When only two months old, the yearling doe had been attacked by a bobcat. Although deformed in the shoulder, the deer had somehow survived the past four months.

The doe headed towards Red Creek, with the coywolf close behind. In panic, the whitetail leaped off the bank into the raging waters. Both animals were swept downstream. The coywolf caught up with the deer, and managed to clamp her jaws onto a hind leg just as the torrent carried them over a steep drop. The plunge entrapped the young coywolf beneath a submerged log. Death came quickly.

BEAR HOUNDS

One morning in November, the pack was sleeping in a pine stand. They had covered 14 miles the previous night, unsuccessfully pursuing three different deer. They did kill an adult beaver towards morning, however. Fifty pounds of beaver filled their stomachs, and they slept soundly throughout the day.

A flock of migrating whistling swans emitted their strange, high-pitched honking while flying high above—headed for their wintering grounds along the Chesapeake Bay. A pair of ravens issued their unique raucous croak, searching for a carcass of an unlucky deer or snowshoe hare. The pack heard these and other sounds that floated overhead, but none intimated danger or the promise of food. Thus, they ignored the sounds and they enjoyed their mid-day naps.

Suddenly Adirondus and Alghena jumped to their feet and the pups raised their heads. Alghena whined anxiously, as the hair on her back raised slightly. The pups became nervous and eased closer towards Alghena. Their acute hearing picked up distant baying dogs heading in their direction.

The hounds were in pursuit of a black bear. Earlier in the morning bear hunters had driven the Dolly Sods Road (FR 75). The majority of their hounds rode inside travel kennels, but three sensitive-nosed hounds rode on a platform on top of the kennels. The two trucks moved slowly in hopes that one of these "strike" hounds would pick up the scent of a bear.

It was not actually hunting season for black bears, but it was training season for hounds. In Tucker County, bear firearms season was legal for one week in September and for three weeks in December. During those two periods, it was legal to kill a bear—and to pursue them with hounds. To train young hounds and get mature hounds back into physical condition, hunters were provided the opportunity to pursue bears with hounds at any time of the year, although they could not have firearms in their possession.

Hunters with young dogs had begun "obedience" training in early summer, so that by September the youngsters were comfortable with a leash, riding in the dog kennel in a bouncing pickup truck, with wearing two or three collars, and with being around as many as a dozen other hounds. The young hounds had also been trained to trail the scent given off by a piece of raccoon hide that had been soaked in bear scent.

"Byrd," one of the hounds, suddenly began barking wildly; he had picked up the fresh scent of a black bear. Byrd, a brown brindle Plott, who weighed 60 pounds, was so excited he strained against his chain in the kennel box. A light misty rain had fallen the previous night, creating ideal scenting conditions. A young male bear, about 18 months old, had crossed the road less than 20 minutes earlier that morning. The pickup trucks came to a halt, and the men hustled to the tailgates.

Byrd bounced off the tailgate, and excitedly crisscrossed the road several times before deciding the bear had headed west. With non-stop barking, he crossed a small ditch and disappeared into the woods. The bear and its direction of travel were confirmed through his tracks.

The other hounds were released and in minutes 11 dogs were tearing across the plateau. Three of the hounds were Plotts, five were black and tan coonhounds, two were Walkers, and one was a bluetick coonhound. Each could run a scent trail nonstop for hours at a time.

Adirondus and the pack were nearly a mile away. They were not alarmed, but he listened intently, while Alghena let out an anxious whine.

The yearling black bear also heard the barking, and broke into a rambling gallop. The bear was in excellent condition and capable of running 30 miles per hour for long distances. In contrast, hounds would seldom exceed 20 miles per hour. Whereas the bear could run at his top speed, slowing only to avoid obstacles, the hounds frequently lost the bear's scent and spent many minutes picking up the trail again.

The bear headed southwest, following a rocky streambed before reaching the junction of Fisher Spring Run and Red Creek. The hounds had no difficulty following the bear's scent along Fisher Spring Run, but lost his trail in the small boulders and pools of deep water in Red Creek. They lost nearly 20 minutes searching for where the bear had exited the stream. But the bear's scent was strong enough that the dogs' excited barking never stopped.

The hounds' owners, meanwhile, waited at their pickup trucks. The men could identify the voice of each of his hounds, and the constant barking alerted them to the general direction they traveled. The owners also had a virtual "image" of almost the exact path being taken. Each hound wore a GPS collar that transmitted direction, speed, and distance. The men were observing the chase on a monitor, mapping progress atop contour lines, roads, and streams. Each hound was tracked by a uniquely colored moving line, which also had the name of the hound.

The men never knew how far ahead the bear was until the dogs forced the bear to climb a tree. With the hounds clustered around the base of the tree, the monitor would reveal that the bear was treed. Bear hunters rarely used fewer than 12 hounds in a chase, to reduce the chance a bear might stop running and fight the hounds.

The bear followed Red Creek, and with the barking faded slightly, he plopped into a small pool. He relaxed, drank his fill, and listened to his pursuers non-stop barking.

Adirondus' concern heightened when the chorus rolled up the mountainside directly towards their lookout site. The coywolves had moved to a small opening on the ridgeline and spotted the bear, but they made no effort to run. Only when Adirondus spotted the hounds along the streambed did he signal his pack to follow. He led them to a hiking trail and followed it towards the east. They loped steadily away from the hounds.

The bear exited the pool, climbed the high bank and headed up the hillside. By chance, he was headed directly to where the coywolf pack had witnessed the chase. And, by chance alone, the bear turned southeast towards Fisher Spring Run where he followed the hiking trail for a short distance. Bear tracks mingled with coywolf tracks on the muddy trail. Meanwhile, the hounds lost the bear scent at the pool and spent 15 minutes soaking, drinking, and resting just as the bear had.

Adirondus and the pack followed Fisher Spring Trail for about a half mile, headed in a northeasterly direction. The bear followed the hiking trail southwest. When the hounds resumed their chase, they also eventually reached the Fisher Spring hiking trail. Noses poring over the surface, they were distracted by the strange new scent. The bear chase was suddenly altered, and two of the young hounds followed the trail of the coywolves.

Hearing the new pattern of barking, Adirondus changed his pace from a steady trot to a slow gallop and soon broke into a large marshy area that contained several large beaver ponds. With no hesitation, he plunged in and all pack members swam across the pond.

The two young hounds, named Julie and Nancy, reached the beaver pond but lost the scent. They could hear the other hounds, but their minds were consumed by the fresh scent of the coywolves. Meanwhile the hunters were monitoring both the youngsters and the other hounds. They had no way of knowing what scent the young hounds were following, but they knew it was not that of the bear.

In addition to a GPS collar, each young hound wore a shock collar that had a range of slightly over one mile. Realizing the shock collar was likely out of range, the owner jumped into his Dodge Ram and hustled to the trailhead of Fisher Spring Trail. He flipped the switches that triggered a short burst of electricity into the neck of each hound. Both yipped, and with the second electrical shock abandoned the coywolf chase. Half an hour later, they had rejoined the other hounds.

One of the two young hounds was also equipped with a GoPro camera attached to a specially designed vest. The camera was transmitting to a smartphone to monitor progress, but the owner was too far away to receive the video. The camera contained a memory card so the travels of the hound could be reviewed later. They could evaluate the performances of the two young hounds that evening at home.

The bear reached Rhorbaugh Plains Trail, which he followed south. Continuing around the hillside he reached the upper end of a deep gully. There he rested for several minutes before dropping into the gulley. The hounds were rapidly gaining on the bear, and as he began his descent, the hounds caught sight of him. They began trailing visually, and with the hounds less than a football field away the bear shimmied up a large red maple. There he remained, while the hounds leaped high off the ground against the tree trunk in a frantic attempt to climb the tree.

The men, breathing heavily, arrived within 40 minutes, having hustled on foot across Rhorbaugh Plains. Admiring and then video-taping the young bear, they attached leashes to the hounds and began the hike back to the trucks. As soon as they passed out of sight, the bear carefully scooted rump first down the tree. Had the chase occurred during the gun season in December, the outcome would have been drastically different.

A Colorless Landscape

By mid-November, multiple freezes and occasional light snowfalls had brought to an end the autumn glory that attracted so many tourists. To the color-blind coyotes/coywolves, visibility beneath stands of hardwoods increased, as more light reached the forest floor.

The dark fur coats of Adirondus and Applacha enabled them to blend closely with the dark stumps and surroundings. When the ground was without snow, they were so camouflaged they could glide unseen while searching for prey. The reddish-tan coats of Alghena and her other offspring had enabled them to blend in closely with vegetative cover dominated by grasses, ferns, and goldenrod during summer months, but they lost some of that advantage during winter months.

Frogs, toads, salamanders, and turtles, plus bats, groundhogs, and many female black bears had entered hibernation by November. Most songbirds had departed for warmer climates. Canada geese and a few wood ducks remained, but the first heavy cold front out of Canada would hasten their departure.

Amidst the exodus, certain migrants had only just arrived. Numerous waterfowl would stop in the Valley on their way south. Diving ducks, including mergansers, scaup, and bufflehead would rest on beaver ponds, as would dabblers such as black ducks, pintails, and widgeons.

One avian migrant numbered in the tens of thousands. Northern cold fronts propelled thousands of the stubby, quail-sized American woodcocks into Canaan Valley. These brought hundreds of hunters and their pointing dogs.

Woodcock and grouse were of little direct importance to coywolves. They were rarely captured, and they provided little nourishment. But they attracted an influx of human hunters. Throughout the four week hunting season there were more humans and dogs than at any other time of the year.

Bow season for deer typically opened by the first week of October, and trapping for furbearers opened the first week of November. In addition, waterfowl hunters and turkey hunters frequented wetland and wooded habitats. Hunting was not allowed in Timberline or Canaan Valley State Park. But, it was allowed in Canaan Valley National Wildlife Refuge and most areas of Dolly Sods. That included Dolly Sods Wilderness (but not Dolly Sods Scenic Area) and all other lands within the Monongahela National Forest.

Because of the human hunting, Adirondus and his pack moved south of FR 19. Several large stands of conifers had been planted here by the CCC (Civilian Conservation Corps) in the 1930s. Another unique feature that attracted coywolves and humans was a complex of shallow man-made potholes south of the picnic area. These had been blasted by the WVDNR in the 1960s and 1970s, in an attempt to create additional habitat for wetland wildlife. Woodcock and grouse frequented the dense woody cover around the potholes.

Social changes were occurring in the pack. Adirondus was becoming aggressive towards his male offspring, with snarling and occasional nipping. Two of the juvenile males began hunting together, often wandering several miles from the main pack. They also began hunting during daylight hours.

In early November, the two juveniles were trotting around the hillside above Red Creek. A bow hunter was sitting in his tree stand when he spotted the pair. He was shivering from the freezing wind and had not seen a deer all day. When one of the pups stopped to examine the doe-urine bait, the frustrated hunter leveled the sights of his compound bow onto the shoulder of the coywolf and released a three bladed aluminum arrow. The arrow sliced through his heart, and the coywolf took only a few steps before dropping dead.

The other pup never heard the bow or the arrow, only the sudden "wuff" of his brother. He ran a short distance, before stopping behind a red maple. The bowhunter carefully lowered his bow with a nylon cord, then slowly descended the stand. Watching the hunter approach his dead brother, the surviving brother sprinted towards the cover of a dense mountain laurel thicket.

That coywolf, named "Montiva", spent nearly an hour in the thicket, before hunger drove him to continue hunting. For the first time in his life, he was alone. However, the memory of an aggressive Adirondus drove Montiva to search for food rather than for his pack. For four days, he found nothing to eat, but on the fifth day he discovered the skeleton of another hunter-killed deer. Unfortunately, little remained other than skull and bones. The coywolf shattered the ends of several rib bones, but obtained only tidbits of marrow.

With a sudden weather shift, a heavy snowstorm blew as Montiva continued hunting. Snow stopped falling before daylight, then Montiva saw a barbed wire fence of a farm bordering Lanesville Road.

Prominently silhouetted against the glistening snow, several hundred yards below, was a small herd of black angus cattle. Montiva sat on his haunches and studied the cattle for nearly an hour. Most were too large to attack, but one appeared similar in size to a large white-tailed buck. That calf had been born months later than the other calves so the farmer had not included it with the other calves when he shipped them to market.

The cows began bawling when Montiva crawled beneath the barbed wire. Although only seven months old, Montiva weighed 50 pounds, slightly more than his mother. The calf weighed 280 pounds, but in contrast to the 1,500-pound cows and the 2,000-pound bull it looked small enough for Montiva to attack—at least from a distance. Montiva moved towards the cattle, making no effort to hide as he crossed the pasture. The cows nervously moved closer together, but the calf remained visible.

At 60 yards, Montiva broke into a slow trot, his gaze fixed directly upon the calf. Most large carnivores avoid chasing healthy, adult animals for fear of injury. Potential prey are typically forced to run so the coywolves can spot any individual restricted in its movements. Targeting a handicapped animal will make it easier and safer for coywolves to bring one down. Adirondus had taught his offspring to test deer in this way, and they rarely pursued large bucks, or even mature does.

Montiva was hungry however, and hunger forced him to take chances. Just 20 yards away, Montiva yipped and the cows began to run. This close, Montiva realized the calf was considerably larger than he was, and it was unlikely he could actually bring it down. He slowed, but continued his pursuit as the cattle ran towards the barn.

Alarmed by the commotion, the farmer exited the barn and immediately spotted the rusty-brown canine. Rob O'Donnell had worked the family farm for nearly his entire life and had suffered numerous losses from predators. He had raised sheep during the 1970s, but eventually abandoned that due to kills by black bears, bobcats, and feral hounds. Had coyotes been in the region then, they would have forced O'Donnell to abandon his sheep operations even earlier.

O'Donnell at first thought the animal was a German shepherd that had wandered onto his farm. As Montiva loped closer, O'Donnell realized his shape differed drastically from a shepherd. He quickly returned to the barn, grabbed the .30-30 Marlin rifle he kept handy for shooting groundhogs, and ran back outside. Raising the rifle, he aimed for the shoulder of the running coywolf and hurriedly shot. Had

Montiva been sitting and the farmer braced the rifle, the 100-grain bullet would have ended Montiva's life. As fate would have it, the bullet barely grazed the skin over his shoulder, and caused no serious damage.

At the rifle's crack, Montiva instantly forgot his "attack" on the cattle, and sprinted at 35 miles per hour towards the treeline. With disgust, the farmer regretted not keeping his 12-gauge shotgun loaded and handy.

Montiva ran a mile before stopping in a rhododendron thicket where he remained until darkness. With a pair of barred owls exchanging messages, he headed to the Canaan Valley State Park ski complex. Driven by hunger, Montiva was drawn to numerous trash cans. All had a bear-proof design, and thus were definitely coywolf-proof. Although a coywolf might have been more intelligent than a black bear, it had neither the strength nor the dexterity in its paws to gain access.

Three days later, Sean, the son of the farmer who had sent Montiva racing, arrived home from Virginia Tech. It was Thanksgiving week, and deer gun season had opened that Monday. On Thanksgiving morning, Sean eased out of the farmhouse with a .30-06 rifle and worked his way into the woods. His dad had described the incident involving their cattle, so Sean was alert for either deer or "dog" tracks.

Sean discovered tracks left by Montiva and followed them towards Canaan Valley State Park. Confident the tracks would lead him into the red spruce thickets surrounding the upper chair lift, he selected a blown-down red maple for a ground blind and placed his insulated cushion at the base of the tree trunk. With insulated clothing and a thermos of hot tea, he waited. By mid-afternoon he abandoned the hunt and returned home for the family Thanksgiving dinner.

Canaan Valley State Park provided little food for a solitary coywolf as November gave way to December. Deer were abundant, but Montiva was not large enough to bring down a healthy adult. Montiva returned to Dolly Sods, and during the next week he ate only two meadow voles and the shriveled carcass of a young wild turkey.

Then his luck changed. While in a rhododendron thicket, he caught the odor of a dead deer. The small buck had been shot by a bow hunter, but ran 400 yards before crawling into the thicket. It died three days later. Cool weather preserved its flesh, and the dense thicket hid it from view of any crows, ravens, or vultures that might fly over. Montiva remained near the steadily dwindling carcass for over two weeks.

Sean O'Donnell spent the ensuing Christmas vacation at home. His father said that dog-like tracks had twice again appeared in the pasture. Although the cattle had not been harassed, Rob O'Donnell was concerned that the canine might still be in the area when calves were dropped in the spring. Rob asked his son to trap or shoot the animal while he was home.

The family owned six #2, Victor double coil padded foothold traps that Sean meticulously set just outside the barbed wire fence. Using artificial coyote lure, he strategically placed the traps near trails. The traps, having been boiled in baking soda and soaked in water containing spruce twigs, were stained a dark black, and blended closely with the soil.

The traps were concealed beneath loamy soil in shallow depressions, the accompanying chain being attached to a sunken metal anchor. Sean wore rubber gloves and rubber boots to contain his scent, and wore outer clothing that had been kept in a scent-free bag, as well as having been saturated with a scent-eliminating spray.

Montiva typically visited the O'Donnell farm once every five or six days on a 24-mile hunting circuit. During the last week of December, he neared the O'Donnell farm and smelled the coyote urine that Sean had sprinkled on the pans of the traps. Curiosity drew Montiva to the site. However, human scent became apparent as he approached a buried trap. Sean had used an old burlap bag to haul his traps, plus a well-worn small shovel to prepare the set.

Montiva's parents had taught their pups to avoid any area heavy with human scent. Montiva cautiously circled the area where the trap was buried. Concerned, but not frightened, the coywolf stepped closer. Suddenly the jaws were released from the metal pan. Montiva sprung backwards, his right front foot struck a glancing blow by one of the steel jaws. Whether by chance or from caution, rather than setting his foot onto the pan he had placed his weight on one of the metal jaws.

Montiva quickly left, but encountered another trap as he worked his way around the hill. He approached within seven yards but went no closer. Schooling by his parents—and now his own near miss—had taught him that human scent was usually associated with danger.

A light snow had fallen a few hours after Sean had set the traps, and tracks in the snow now told an interesting story. The large tracks showed four distinct toes and a prominent heel pad. Each three inches wide and slightly more so in length—nearly the size typical of a cougar or a wolf. Sean knew with certainty they were not made by the cat family as the claw marks were quite prominent. Also, no cougars had been spotted in the area for over 50 years. But he was also aware that no wolves had been reported in over 100 years.

One of the gifts Sean received from his father that Christmas was an electronic game call. When he failed to catch anything in his steel traps after five days, he made plans to try out the battery-powered game call. The previous October, he had constructed a ground blind that was high enough that he could solidly rest his rifle on a limb. Through openings, the blind provided shots in three directions. The woods were relatively open and he could easily see an approaching animal at distances up to 150 yards.

Sean entered the blind the morning of New Year's Day, having first concealed the game call 125 yards down the hill. The call was camouflaged with red spruce boughs, and the loudspeaker was aimed away from the blind. Anxious to begin, Sean pushed several buttons on the remote which triggered a squealing rabbit from the game call's speaker. The remote had a functional distance of 200 yards.

The device had over 150 pre-installed animal calls, giving Sean more options than he would possibly use. Another gift he received for Christmas was a bottle of odor-free detergent and a can of scent-eliminating spray. Using them, he felt confident nothing would pick up his odor.

A clean blanket of snow covered the forest that New Year's day. Sean wore all-white coveralls and a white toboggan. Only a light breeze moved up the hill, confirming his belief that his detectability was quite low. He set the game call to repeat the distressed rabbit cry every 17 minutes.

Nearly an hour after climbing into this ground blind, Sean saw a red fox slipping through the trees, heading directly towards the speaker. He had a clear shot and brought the cross hairs to rest at the top of the animal's left shoulder. The distance was a little over 100 yards, and by holding his sights a little high, he was confident the bullet would strike a vital organ.

But rather than squeezing off a shot, he relaxed and slipped his finger from the trigger. Although foxes had killed a couple of their free-ranging chickens in recent years, Sean believed they ate enough rodents and rabbits to more than cover the value of a couple chickens. And if the fox killed only one groundhog per year, it would have a positive impact on their cattle operation. Besides, Sean was after larger prey that day.

The previous night, Sean had been to a party in Harman, and he now caught himself dozing. It was after a catnap that he spotted a distant canine slowly easing its way around a mountain laurel bush. Gently he raised his Remington .30-06. In the still air, Montiva had heard the rabbit squeals from two miles away. At 300 yards, he stopped, crouched low to the ground, and carefully searched the hillside from where the squeals seemed to originate. Spotting nothing suspicious, he continued his slow advance.

When he was 75 yards away, Sean squeezed the trigger. Montiva heard the explosion but he had no time to react. The bullet struck slightly behind his shoulder blade, then went through both lungs, assuring he would never be hungry again.

Because of its large size and wolf-like features, Sean took the carcass back to Blacksburg, where he showed it to a professor in the Wildlife Program. The Virginia Tech professor was certain the animal had wolf ancestry, but offered to conduct a mitochondrial DNA analysis to obtain a positive identity. He explained it was not the first hybrid canine collected in the area. A previous study directed by a biologist in nearby Christiansburg had documented the presence of four, coyote-like animals with significant Algonquin wolf ancestry from western Virginia.

ANOTHER MATING SEASON

In mid-winter, Adirondus began acting aggressive towards his one remaining male offspring, Tuckerus. Just as Adirondus' father had driven him from the pack's territory, Adirondus growled and snarled daily at his one surviving son, even inflicting painful nips to his rump. One night during a February hunt, Adirondus prevented Tuckerus from joining him, Alghena, and the two surviving female pups, Applacha and Estrella. Tuckerus hunted alone, but four days later he was allowed to rejoin the pack.

Adirondus, Alghena, and their three remaining offspring remained on the southern end of Dolly Sods all winter. One afternoon in March, Alghena discovered a groundhog burrow. She was once again pregnant, and the urge was strong to prepare a den for her next litter. Alghena dug for two hours while Adirondus and his three offspring hunted around the potholes that had been blasted by the WVDNR. They captured a skinny groundhog that had emerged from hibernation, and then they aroused a bedded, yearling buck.

The young buck had been wounded in November by a bullet, which passed cleanly through his left shoulder. The wound had healed but muscle damage handicapped its movements. It survived the deep snows of winter but lost considerable weight.

They were nearly three miles from Alghena and close behind the buck, when a black bear discovered the fresh soil Alghena had removed

from the old groundhog den. The three-year-old male bear tipped the
scales at 280 pounds even after emerging from a 3-month hibernation.
Ravenous, he would eat almost anything he discovered. However, few
foods were present in March.

Given the choice, the bear would have been better off waiting until
April to emerge from his den. Now awake and famished, the combined
odor of groundhog and coyote were too tempting for the bear to pass up.
He had widened the burrow four feet before Alghena became aware of
his presence.

Most groundhog dens contain both a main entrance and a secondary,
escape route. Alghena had encountered a root nearly halfway down the
main entrance. She could push her head past the root, but her shoulders
would not pass. She was trapped! The coyote dug frantically to widen
the passage. Time, however, was seriously limited. Clawing rapidly in the
dark tunnel, she howled in panic, calling for her mate, but to no avail.

The black bear dug for 50 minutes before hooking his two-inch long
front claws into Alghena. He eased back out of the burrow and brought
the screaming coyote with him. His jaws closed around her hips and she
was instantly paralyzed. Another bite, and death soon followed.

Adirondus and his three pups killed the buck and within an hour
had filled their stomachs. The four canines moved a short distance away
and were soon sleeping. Normally they would have remained and eaten
again the next morning, but Adirondus was driven to respond to the
needs of his mate. While Applacha, Estrella, and their brother, Tuckerus,
remained asleep, their father awoke and began the return trip to feed
Alghena. He would regurgitate chunks of fresh meat to her at the new
den site.

Adirondus discovered the few broken bones and pieces of fur that
the bear had discarded, along Alghena's scent in the burrow. He quickly
found the bear digging up roots of skunk cabbage several hundred yards
away. He made several futile attacks, but was no match for a full-grown

bear. Even with his surviving offspring, he would not have persisted in attacking.

He returned to the place of death, and searched the surrounding hillsides for his mate. After two days, he returned to the deer carcass and rejoined his son and two daughters. Although little meat remained, Adirondus spent much of the next day gnawing on bones and eating marrow and cartilage.

PACK DEMISE

The four-member pack hunted together throughout March, but the bond was weakening. Wolves have a strong urge to belong to a pack, while coyotes prefer a solitary life. Had Adirondus, Applacha, Estrella, and Tuckerus been pure-blooded wolves they would have likely stayed together and slowly added other pack members.

Adirondus began hunting alone most nights, and by May, he had totally abandoned his offspring. He wandered north and was drawn to where he had mated with Alghena and assisted in raising the pups. He knew exactly where the den was located. He utilized odors, contours of the terrain, drainage patterns of small streams, and at times, the stars overhead. Wolves, coyotes, and coywolves exhibit the remarkable ability to hunt over a 20 square-mile area and then return unerringly to their den.

Adirondus spent weeks near the old den, and on several occasions he crawled into it. By May, humans in the area caused Adirondus to move on and search for a new mate. Dobbins Slashing Bog became the center of his home range, and for the remainder of that year he lived a solitary life.

In February, Adirondus picked up the alluring scent of a female coyote. As he searched, his excitement rose. In less than an hour he spotted her. He sat on his haunches, studying the coyote as she searched around a small beaver pond for meadow voles.

A slow trot brought Adirondus within 40 yards of the coyote before she saw him. Dropping to her belly in the glistening snow, she studied Adirondus as he slowed his stalk. At 10 yards, he halted and dropped to his belly. They studied each other for several minutes, then Adirondus gave out a playful yip. A whine from the female provided all the encouragement he needed, and he bounded towards her. Alarmed, she galloped away. Adirondus slowly followed, and 20 minutes later the two were exchanging intimate sniffs and lip licks. Both were anxious to find a companion.

The two-year-old coyote had abandoned her family as she entered her first estrus period. Her mother had become belligerent towards her and the other two offspring and ran them off as she herself was again entering estrus

Nearly 20 pounds lighter than Adirondus, she nevertheless showed no fear of him. The two mated in late February, and in April she gave birth to five healthy pups. Adirondus resumed the role of dedicated father and kept his mate, his pups, and himself well fed.

Following the departure of Adirondus, his three siblings hunted together, but pack cohesiveness weakened daily. One day in April, Estrella wandered away from her siblings. Had Alghena continued nursing a litter of pups, the yearling would have assisted in their upbringing. Now she felt no connection to her other pack members. Instead, instinct spurred her on, and she trotted casually to the north, following FR 75, up the eastern edge of the Dolly Sods plateau.

On the second day alone, Estrella reached the Red Creek Campground near the Brooks Bird Club Bird Banding Station. Snowdrifts remained, preventing most humans from venturing into the wilderness area. Meadow voles were abundant enough to take the edge off her hunger.

One evening Estrella spotted a mid-sized animal in the campgrounds. It was a red fox. Her father had taught her to kill all foxes, and she easily approached within 12 yards of the fox. The fox was behaving oddly, snarling and stumbling, but this was of little significance to Estella. She pounced when the fox meandered within striking distance. It was an easy kill.

A two-year-old male coyote born near Winchester, Virginia, had just wandered nearby on his journeys. The husky coyote, whose lineage included a Canadian wolf, had followed the faint scent of the red fox for nearly an hour, and had closed to within 200 yards when Estrella made her kill. He heard the scream of the dying fox and galloped towards it. Estrella was not aware of the coyote until snarls revealed his presence ten yards away.

She was slightly smaller than the coyote, but she had no intention of abandoning her kill. She ate her fill of the 20-pound fox before moving off some 40 yards and allowing the male to eat.

The two gradually formed a close-knit pair, and a month later they were cooperating on successful hunts. Their home range extended from the eastern edge of the Dolly Sods plateau to the South Branch of the Potomac River. In February, about ten months after meeting the male coyote, Estrella enlarged a den at the base of a large complex of boulders, east of the Red Creek Campground. In March, she gave birth to four pups.

Applacha and Tuckerus had developed into a highly efficient hunting team. One evening they were east of the White Grass Cross Country Ski Area when the smell of white-tailed deer flesh flooded their nostrils. Applacha took the lead, and circled downwind. They were within 25 yards when they pinpointed the deer. As confirmation, they picked up the gnashing of teeth and the snarls of a fox. Fearing nothing, Applacha bounded in long strides towards the carcass. The fox barely escaped with its life.

Both coywolves were tearing off large chunks of meat when a light suddenly illuminated the area. They jumped backwards but remained a few feet from the deer. When no other disturbance occurred, they cautiously returned to their feast. Two minutes later, a flash of light again pierced the darkness. Again, the coywolves ceased feeding. This happened four times before Applacha ignored the light and continued feasting.

Applacha and Tuckerus were being photographed by a remote game camera attached to a nearby spruce by a biologist from the Canaan Valley National Wildlife Refuge. The goal was to analyze golden eagles on Dolly Sods. These large predatory birds follow the Appalachian Mountains during their annual migration, and a few are winter residents.

The two coywolves satiated their hunger, wiped their faces in snow to remove the blood. The next day they would compete with a golden eagle for the remaining flesh. The research ended in April, and the coywolves discovered there were no more free meals provided by Refuge biologists.

Their feeding forays eventually led them far to the north, into Canaan Valley. Spring gobbler season opened the last week of April and extended until the middle of May. After two encounters with hunters, the coywolves began avoiding wooded areas. Applacha and Tuckerus concentrated on the open areas along Glade Run and Sand Run.

One night in early May, they moved across the emergency spillway of Sand Run Lake dam and searched the eastern perimeter of the lake that was occupied by eight cabins. Applacha and Tuckerus were after meadow voles. These lemming-like rodents had produced a litter the previous month, the first of seven litters that year. Numerous weaned youngsters were exploring their grassy world. Tuckerus heard the squeaks of a juvenile vole, his erect ears pinpointing its exact location, and he pounced high in the air before dropping directly onto it. Applacha was on the opposite side of the stream and watched in envy as her brother quickly gulped down the vole.

A hundred yards further on, Applacha crouched low in the marsh grass, and emitted a low, almost imperceptible whimper. Tuckerus halted and studied his sibling for further guidance. Applacha moved forward, her belly sliding through the damp grass. After progressing eight yards at a near snail's pace, Applacha suddenly sprang from the grass. She heard the bones crunching and the strong odor of a mink. She struck the mink, but made no effort to kill the brown-pelted member of the weasel family. Applacha was focused on its meal, a large fish.

The fish was a white sucker, which had been working its way up Sand Run in search of a spot to lay her eggs. Other white suckers were making the same trip, including several males that would fertilize the eggs. The fish was nine inches long, and weighed nearly a pound.

Without hesitation Applacha ripped off chunks of fish. Tuckerus quickly crossed the small stream and attempted to snatch a bite of fish, but Applacha curled back her lips, exposed her dagger-like teeth, and snarled menacingly.

Unable to resist, Tuckerus dashed in and grabbed the fish's tail as Applacha was gnawing on the head. The backbone separated, and each coywolf ended up with a portion of the fish. Applacha crushed and swallowed the entire head, including the thick lips so characteristic of white suckers. Tuckerus obtained little nourishment from the bones and tail but relished the flavor.

The 80-acre alder swamp along the headwaters of Sand Run supported numerous prey. Applacha and Tuckerus learned to focus their hunting on the goldenrod fields between the lakeshore and the vacation houses. The two developed a hunting strategy of moving slowly, about 15 yards apart. Any fawn that twitched an ear, flicked a tail, or jumped up and attempted to escape was readily seen and captured.

FAST FOOD

Several nights in May, when the moon was full, Applacha initiated a series of barks, howls, and yips. Tuckerus, with his nose pointed skyward, joined in. The chorus of drawn-out, wavering howls and yelps/yips was intermixed with occasional barking and high-pitched wailing. Nothing in particular triggered the "singing" and most likely, even the coywolves did not know why they sang. Possibly they were lonely and wanted to contact other so called "songdogs." More likely, their vocalizations strengthened social bonds between them, and announced their territory.

They varied their modulation and intensity to such an extent that the serenade sounded like five to ten individuals were contributing. Coyotes are capable of producing at least 14 different vocalizations: growl, huff, woof, bark, bark-howl, wail, whine, yelp, woo-oo-wow, lone howl, group howl, group yip-howl, whoop, and yodel.

Humans can hear a coyote howl at a distance of up to five miles. Coyote serenades are described as eerie, dismal, gay, gladsome, hideous, hilarious, maniacal, mournful, scornful, and unearthly. J. Frank Dobie [The Voice of the Coyote] wrote, "If I could, I would go to bed every night with coyote voices in my ears and with them greet the gray light of every dawn."

Applacha and her brother frequently engaged in the yip-howl serenade on clear starlit nights. Their communiques caused messages on the internet warning homeowners about the threats of coyotes. One message recommended that cats and small dogs should be kept in the house.

During June, Applacha and her brother crossed Timberline Road, and moved around Spruce Island Lake. There they captured a young beaver where the lake's outflow entered Yoakum Run. They then reached the North Branch of the Blackwater River. The stream, while a river in name, was narrow enough that the coywolves hunted on opposite sides of the stream. One morning they spotted an opossum-sized critter with black and white patches that had a long tail. It resembled a striped skunk, an animal intimately familiar to the coywolves.

Although aware the spray would burn their eyes for minutes, the hungry coywolves reflexively moved 15 yards apart to begin their stalk. They soon realized the prey was not a skunk, but a housecat, named Cedrick. It had been let out at daylight, as was the custom. The long-haired cat hunted every morning, frequently capturing a small rodent or songbird—sometimes eaten but other times left on the doorstep for his owner.

This morning, Cedrick had captured a young ruffed grouse. The cat had discovered the mother grouse and her family of nine chicks at the edge of a viburnum thicket. The female grouse's first clutch of eggs had been eaten by a marauding raccoon, and these chicks were her second clutch. The mother grouse had flushed when the cat came close. Some of the young ran a short distance and crouched in the ground cover, while the more developed flew up into the low branches of a shrub.

Cedrick was an excellent hunter. The tomcat, with tail twitching and front feet trembling, eased forward. At two feet, the grouse sprang into flight, but the cat swiped and sank his claws into the bird's back. Cat and grouse fell to the ground in a pile of fur and feathers. Two bites later, the bird was dead. Cedrick got a good grip and began the trip back to his house.

Applacha and Tuckerus stalked within 20 feet before the distracted cat discovered their presence and broke into a bounding sprint to a nearby tree. The distance was too great, and the coywolves too fast. Minutes later, Applacha was feasting on Frisky-fattened cat, while her brother quickly consumed the young grouse.

After the tasty meal, the coywolves continued westward and reached State Rt. 32, the main highway running north-south through Canaan Valley. Several cars passed before Applacha selected a silent interval to dash across the asphalt. Tuckerus hesitated, but followed shortly behind.

Canaan Valley State Park provided more of a refuge for the coywolves than the wildlife refuge. Hunting, trapping, and training bear dogs were not permitted in the park, whereas they were in the refuge proper. Deer in Canaan Valley State Park had lost much of their natural wariness. In addition, many visitors fed deer even though such feeding was prohibited. Consequently, due to overpopulation, deer in the park were smaller and less healthy than throughout the refuge. Geese and groundhogs were also more abundant in the park due to the ponds and mowed golf course

In Canaan Valley, Canada geese returned from wintering in the coastal Carolinas by March, at about the same time groundhogs were emerging from hibernation. Geese soon paired off, built nests, laid eggs, and by June were attempting to bring their goslings to maturity. The opportunistic coywolves regularly searched through the mowed fields. As a result, throughout June their diet varied widely, combining careless geese and groundhogs with muskrats and meadow voles, opossums and raccoons, and eggs of birds and snapping turtles.

As they foraged around stream and pond edges Applacha and Tuckerus grew comfortable including the cluster of park cabins in their nightly circuit. Twenty-three cabins were available for rent. Trash cans and small dumpsters were present, but not all food scraps ended up in the cans. Bones, apple cores, partially-eaten sandwiches, and numerous other goodies were discovered by Applacha and Tuckerus.

However, the coywolves had to compete with other wildlife for the food scraps. White-tailed deer, raccoons, and opossums had long ago learned to visit each cabin nightly. Feeding wildlife was prohibited but some park guests still put food outside cabins so they could observe and photograph wildlife.

Although "table scraps" did not harm Applacha and Tuckerus, they resulted in the siblings associating humans with food. Absent that fear, the coywolves began approaching ever closer—like other wildlife. The threat of dangerous conflicts with humans increased, and in one instance, the WVDNR was called to remove a bear that became habituated to humans near cabins. To underscore the problem, the WVDNR posted signs that read, "A Fed Bear is a Dead Bear."

The overall impact of humans feeding wildlife may or may not have been beneficial to Applacha and Tuckerus. By July, the coywolves visited the cabins once or twice a week, not so much for the food scraps but for the vulnerable, marauding opossums and raccoons. More than once Tuckerus studied a small boy carrying a bag of trash to the cabin's dumpster. The child was small enough that the coywolf measured him as potential prey. Fortunately for the boy, he was never attacked.

FLANAGAN HILL SHEEP

Applacha and Tuckerus left the State Park by the end of July, when deer fawns were no longer vulnerable and geese had regained their flight ability. They eventually ended up at Flanagan Hill where several farmers raised beef cattle and two raised sheep.

Late one evening the coywolves encountered the fence of William Tuckwiller's farm where a flock of sheep grazed peacefully. Neither Applacha nor Tuckerus had ever seen a sheep, but they somewhat resembled white-tailed deer. Applacha was hesitant to crawl under the fence, but her brother found a depression and slipped beneath. He began working his way down the hill towards the defenseless sheep.

The Tuckwiller flock consisted of 1 ram, 36 ewes, and 30 lambs, all Dorsetts. Tuckerus trotted silently, head low, and was spotted by the sheep 45 yards away. The sheep began bleating and milled around in panic, the predator's presence compressing them into a tightly packed flock. Sheep are defenseless and have no body part that can be used as a weapon, and are not even smart enough to run away from predators. They instinctively clump together when danger appears, often in a corner, where two fences meet.

At a distance of 20 yards, Tuckerus ran towards the flock but focused on a lamb that bolted from the group. The 60-pound youngster ran towards the fence. The other sheep quieted and stared in fascination at the attacking coywolf. Tuckerus reached the lamb and leapt at the animal's throat. The lamb gasped for air and a feeble bleat escaped and then all was silent. The coywolf had made no sounds during the attack.

As Tuckerus began feeding, Applacha eased under the fence, trotted down the hill, and soon was feeding on the heart and lungs. The remainder of the flock resumed grazing, but moved away from the spectacle. The coywolves remained at the carcass for nearly two hours, until gorged.

The next morning, old man Tuckwiller headed to the barn to check on a calf with an injured leg. Before reaching the barn door, he heard a flock of ravens croaking loudly. Peering up the mountainside, he spotted at least 11 of the black birds circling overhead. Brow furrowed, he jumped onto his ATV and bounced uphill through the pasture. Without getting off his ATV, he identified the carcass as one of his young lambs.

There was no evidence of what had killed the lamb. Four of his sheep were killed by predators two years earlier, and so from experience he ruled out a black bear or a bobcat. Black bear, he knew, would have consumed most of the lamb and then carried the carcass into the nearby woods. A bobcat would have been capable of killing the lamb, but could have eaten only half of the carcass. Also, bobcats tend to cover their kill after eating. He dismissed the thought of a mountain lion, because none had been positively identified in the region for several decades.

Tuckwiller had heard coyotes howling on the mountain behind his house several times that spring, and another farmer near Harman lost three sheep in April. A wildlife specialist with the USDA (U.S. Department of Agriculture) was called to investigate and declared the sheep had been killed by coyotes.

William Tuckwiller hurried to call the USDA Wildlife Services office in Elkins. Corbin Justin, a WVU graduate, visited and confirmed the predator was a coyote. Tuckwiller was a participant in the statewide sheep protection program, and annually paid the Tucker County Assessor $1.00 per head of sheep he owned. This payment assured him that a

USDA biologist, at no charge, would remove any predator responsible for attacking his sheep. The USDA Elkins office had been contacted to investigate sheep kills in Randolph and Pocahontas counties earlier that year.

Justin recorded details of the kill and walked the perimeter of the pasture. He located a faint track in a spot of bare earth, confident it had been made by a coyote. Two inches wide by three inches long, the overall shape of the track was oval, and the claw marks left distinct depressions created by sharp nails.

The trapper also located three gaps under the wire mesh fence where a coyote could have entered the pasture. Justin set seven wire snares at various locations, including the three fence gaps. Taking all standard precautions, including not breathing on the snares, Justin was confident his traps would be successful.

In nature, death is ever present. In the words of Ernest Thompson Seton [*Wild Animals I Have Known*], "No (wild) animal dies of old age. Its life has soon or late a tragic end. It is only a question of how long it can hold out against its foes."

Tuckerus had stirred from his daytime nap. He stretched his spine and limbs in a dog-like fashion, yawned, checked the sky for circling vultures, then headed directly for the sheep carcass. When he was about halfway to the pasture, his sister woke and followed. Tuckerus sought the same small gap where he had entered last night. Faint scent left by the trapper mingled with those of the sheep but were of little concern to the coywolf in this landscape of multiple new odors. His attention was directed to the sheep carcass.

The opening of each snare was placed in the precise spot where an entering coyote would place its head. Boiled in baking soda to remove human and metal odor, it was installed wearing rubber boots and leather gloves. The snare was stored in a bag of spruce twigs to further camouflage any odors. The bottom of the snare was set eight inches off the ground, and its circular opening was about ten inches wide. The snare was solidly attached to the bottom wire of the fence and clumps of hay were leaned against the cable to hide it.

As if on cue, Tuckerus stepped exactly where the trapper envisioned, pushing his head through the ten-inch snare opening. As his shoulders met the wire's resistance, the loop cinched around his neck. He howled in fright, and reared backward. The loop closed as Tuckerus struggled to pull loose.

Applacha heard her brother from 150 yards away, and broke into a sprint. Confused by his struggling, she whined nervously, pacing back and forth. As the snare tightened, Tuckerus slowly lost consciousness. Applacha crouched at his side, and whimpered quietly in an attempt to prompt her sibling to flee. She remained at his side throughout the night, until vehicle sounds broke the long stillness.

Applacha retreated to where she could view her brother. She growled as the trapper approached Tuckerus. When the trapper released the snare and picked up the dead animal, Applacha cautiously moved a short distance in his direction. She stared menacingly while the trapper reset his snare. Later that day, she cautiously approached the reset snare, and sniffed for signs of danger. The lingering scent of the trapper and that of her now dead brother were fixed permanently in her memory, and she remained only a few minutes before returning to the woods.

Justin was amazed at the size and weight of the animal. He had captured hundreds of coyotes, but this was easily one of the largest. Even more impressive were its wolf-like features. Before leaving, Justin showed the animal to Tuckwiller and his wife. As if to stave off the question, he added that he would freeze the animal and then have its DNA analyzed. He also indicated he wanted to leave his snares set for at least five more nights.

LIFE ALONE

Applacha moved back into Canaan Valley following the death of her last brother. At 16 months old, she now weighed 55 pounds and had the proportionally longer legs and larger skull of a timber wolf. In June, she began hunting muskrats. She learned to locate their bank dens, typically along streams with high banks. There, muskrats dug a burrow from the water's edge four to five feet upward into the bank. Situated above water level, a den provided space for a pair of muskrats to spend the winter. The coywolf learned to wait patiently at such burrow entrances.

Muskrats fed primarily on roots that grew along the bank. At dusk Applacha worked her way along the water's edge until she detected muskrat odor. She sat patiently until the muskrats departed for their evening forays. As they swam from the den, Applacha slowly inched to the water's edge. After an hour or two spent foraging, muskrats returned to their den. They typically swam on the surface until a few feet from the burrow opening, where they dove to their underwater runway and den entrance.

Applacha pounced high in the air. Although successful only 20 percent of the time, her jaws closed around the back of a muskrat enough times to reward her efforts. A muskrat weighed only three pounds, but provided a substantial meal.

Muskrat hunting frequently resulted in encounters with other predators. Mink and raccoons were both competitors of the coywolf.

Mink focused on muskrats, while raccoons consumed anything from frogs, water snakes, and bird eggs to crawdads.

One night Applacha worked her way up Club Run. That small stream was only ten feet wide and a couple feet deep. The coywolf was scanning the water's edge, moving steadily upstream. After 20 minutes, the scent of fresh blood filtered into her quivering nose. She identified it as a muskrat, but simultaneously identified a mink.

The dark brown mink, a member of the weasel family, had killed a young muskrat as it emerged from its bank den. The sharp teeth of the mink had torn the soft underbelly of the muskrat 15 minutes before Applacha arrived. When Applacha closed to within 12 feet, she crouched. Only two powerful bounds were required before she reached the carcass.

The mink neither heard nor smelled Applacha, but did detect her large airborne mass. The mink leaped into Club Run and dove underwater before swimming frantically downstream. It crawled out of the water on the opposite side and hissed several times in displeasure at losing her hard earned meal. Stealing a meal from another predator was certainly easier than stalking and making the kill yourself.

Another June night, as the deep calls of green frogs floated over the wetlands, Applacha heard splashing at a beaver pond and began an investigation. She knew it meant the presence of potential prey—and probably something larger than a muskrat. A short stalk later, Applacha was within six yards of the splashing, and identified the scent of a foraging raccoon. Her attack was successful and, instead of enjoying a muskrat dinner, she feasted on an 18-pound raccoon.

In September, Applacha supplemented her diet with fruit. Wild apple trees began to drop their gnarly crop, while black cherry fruits peppered the forest floor. On two occasions, she fed under a large cherry tree while a black bear fed improbably high in the upper branches. During daylight hours, wild turkey, ruffed grouse, blue jays, and crows consumed thousands of cherries from the uppermost branches. Deer, raccoons, opossums, and mice joined in after dark. Many were so preoccupied with cherries that they failed to stay alert. Thus, Applacha often had a mixed meal consisting of fruits and flesh.

By October, human hunters once again swarmed the Canaan Valley. Although hunting was prohibited in Canaan Valley State Park, it was permitted in thousands of surrounding acres in the Monongahela National Forest. On a frosty morning, Applacha had a close encounter with a human hunter.

Moving slowly through the trees, the gobbling of a wild turkey caught Applacha's attention. She knew that wild turkeys spent nights high in trees. But she also knew they came down at sunup. On a few occasions while stalking chipmunks she had been frightened by the crashing sounds of a turkey landing nearby.

On this morning, as a gobbler sounded off from high in a tree, Applacha heard a similar gobbling call ahead. She began a stalk toward a black cherry trunk uprooted in a winter storm. It was fully two feet in diameter, and at a distance of only eight feet Applacha detected no odors despite the damp conditions and still air. The turkey in the treetop let out two more gobbles, and within seconds a set of clucks answered from the fallen tree. Applacha leapt and identified a dark form as she landed squarely atop it. She was rewarded with a frightened yell from a human turkey hunter.

The hunter wore a large camouflage net over a heavy canvas hunting coat, and Applacha's teeth, temporarily entangled in the netting, did not penetrate him. The weight of Applacha knocked the hunter to the ground, and he dropped his shotgun. It would have been difficult to determine which of the two hunters was more surprised, the human or the coywolf. Applacha quickly regained her footing and tore off through the dark woods. The hunter retrieved his shotgun and fired a belated shot in her direction out of frustration and fear.

Applacha continued running for five minutes before subconsciously evaluating the attack. She had identified human odor and her fear of humans was reinforced. Most importantly she now associated the odor with the blast of a gun. The now-wiser coywolf would have many other encounters with humans, but none so startling and in such close proximity.

Turkeys became less attractive to Applacha following her incident with the hunter. She learned instead to search for gut piles left by successful bow hunters and for crippled deer or turkey left by the unsuccessful ones. Thus, she actually gained weight during November. By December she weighed 60 pounds and looked more like a wolf than a coyote. Her dark, dense winter coat enhanced her distinct appearance, and the few humans who chanced to glimpse her described her as weighing 100 pounds.

One night in December, a solitary male black bear indirectly provided several meals for Applacha. While hunting she picked up the scent of a gut pile. At the innards she discovered an odor different from a white-tailed deer, but similar enough that Applacha did not hesitate to eat. The large liver and kidneys provided enough meat to satisfy her and she moved a short distance away and was soon sleeping.

The gut pile was that of a black bear itself, which had been killed the previous afternoon by a group of bear hunters and their dogs. Applacha stayed near the remains for two weeks. The bear had put on an additional 60 pounds in preparation for hibernation.

Applacha had no problems satisfying her hunger during the summer and autumn. Whether she could be successful on her own during winter was uncertain. Facing reduced prey, she would go days without eating. It was then that she would typically depend on deer. But Applacha would need several pack members to hunt and kill healthy deer.

When hunting season for deer ended in January, Applacha moved out of Monongahela National Forest and returned to Canaan Valley

State Park. Her hunting then re-centered on the Park's lodge and cabins area. She succeeded in killing three visitor-habituated deer, all of which had been late-born fawns. The human food scraps, supplemented with flesh of other scavenging wildlife, provided a few nourishing meals. But Applacha had begun to lose weight.

As hunger became a constant companion, vague thoughts of sheep drew Applacha southward, towards Flanagan Hill. The coywolf arrived on the Tuckwiller farm as February's first major snow storm blew in. Applacha could see none of the livestock or farm buildings at the fence enclosing the upper pasture. The flock of sheep had been put in the barn the previous night to protect them from the approaching storm.

Doubly cautious, Applacha slowly worked her way around the fence searching for a spot where she might squeeze under. Although no scent of her sibling remained, she remembered the scene of his dying struggles.

In the morning Applacha heard muffled farm sounds. Tuckwiller had opened the barn doors, and his sheep came running out into a pasture. Even though heavy snowflakes were falling, the sheep much preferred being outside. They rushed to two bales of hay and minutes later all were feeding. The sheep were Dorsetts, a breed favored by many mountain farmers for their wool and lambs. The flock was predominantly ewes, most of which were now carrying lambs.

Hunger drove Applacha under the fence at a depression, and she slowly maneuvered towards the angus cattle. Because of their intimidating size, she did not consider them potential prey. She had not eaten in three days, and hunger overcame caution. As the snowstorm came to an end she saw the sheep.

The larger ewes weighed about 180 pounds each, and appeared similar in size to an adult white-tailed deer doe. Applacha was approximately 130 yards from where they fed. Although her dark fur contrasted sharply with the snow, neither sheep nor cattle had apparently spotted her. Slinking forward, at 70 yards Applacha tried to select a target.

The sheep were nearly identical in size, and no one individual caught her attention. Undeterred, she began an attack. She had given out a few yips and closed to within 20 yards when a large white shape suddenly materialized from the flock and rushed directly towards her. For a split second, her mind could not understand—and then she reacted.

The farmer had purchased a pup the previous summer, in an attempt to reduce future losses caused by coyotes, bears, and feral dogs. The Great Pyrenees was introduced to the sheep when it was six weeks old, spending every minute with the flock. Such guard dogs had been successful in reducing or even eliminating attacks by bears and coyotes. Following the sheep attack by Tuckerus, and several kills by bears, the USDA Wildlife Services Division had recommended that Tuckwiller purchase a guard dog. The agency even offered a program through which they contributed to the purchase of the pup.

The pup was never allowed in the farmhouse and was treated more like a sheep than a dog. Whether he believed he was a sheep was uncertain. Despite his young age, he had already successfully driven away black bears. The pup had grown to 100 pounds by February when Applacha appeared. His aggressiveness and vocal intimidation emboldened him to drive away bears weighing three times as much.

Spotting the dog, Applacha retreated. With the barking dog rapidly closing, the coywolf headed for the shallow depression where she had entered the pasture. Tuckwiller had been in the barn when he heard the barking. He quickly grabbed his rifle and ran outside. Although he didn't get off a shot, he witnessed the coyote's escape. The Pyrenees continued barking for 20 minutes, eventually returning to his unconcerned flock.

Tuckwiller called his nearest neighbor who also had a flock of sheep. He explained, "Essie, if you've not already let your sheep out for the day, you should keep them in the barn. My guard dog chased a huge, black coyote out of our sheep pasture a few minutes ago. Fortunately, I'd just let our sheep out of the barn, and the goldang thing didn't kill any."

Essie answered Tuckwiller, "I've already let my sheep out, since I need to be at work in the park lodge by eight o'clock. However, after I lost two sheep in December, I put lithium chloride baits around my sheep pasture. Any approaching coyote should discover those baits before figuring out how to get into my sheep pasture. Thanks for the warning, though."

Following the attack by the guard dog, Applacha spent all day in a thick forest stand overlooking the Tuckwiller farm. Sometime after midnight, she approached the taut sheep fence running around the hillside above the farm of Essie Ammons.

As she walked its perimeter she detected sheep and searched diligently, accelerating her pace until finding a three-inch chunk of meat. Applacha quickly gulped down the meat, swallowing even the hunk of wool that was wrapped around it. She gulped down two more chunks of mutton before locating the head of a dead ewe. She gnawed nearly a pound of frozen flesh from the neck and jaws before the lithium chloride began to take effect.

Essie Ammons had injected large amounts of lithium chloride into mutton and the sheep's head. Nausea swept over Applacha. Within an hour, violent vomiting commenced. Weakened, Applacha wobbled clumsily to the spruce stand, vomiting several more times while attempting to sleep. She was too ill to hunt the following day. Humans would have probably concluded they were dying, but Applacha only knew that something was badly wrong.

The lithium chloride was not intended to kill a predator, only to trigger vomiting and to alter behavior. Applacha survived the bouts of vomiting and associated the condition with sheep. The smell of sheep repulsed her now. Essie had considered putting out true poison, but was concerned about non-target animals that invariably consume such baits.

Two days later, as Applacha's hunger pangs returned with severity, she neared a farm just beyond the Tuckwillers. That farm, owned by

Harrison Oneacre, had no sheep, but supported a flock of Rhode Island red chickens and 35 black angus cattle. He had lost a couple chickens in early November, and spread rat poison around his chicken pen which had stopped the attacks.

By coincidence, a bobcat had circled the chicken coop three times the night before Applacha visited the farm. The farmer had identified its tracks in the snow when he went to gather eggs the next morning. He put out more pelletized rat poison around the pen, and made plans to try to shoot the varmint that evening.

About two hours before dark, Oneacre entered a small ground blind strategically positioned alongside a head-high pile of rocks located just outside his upper pasture fence. He waited patiently, but darkness arrived before any marauding feline did.

Although unlikely to have any more luck the following morning, the farmer was willing to suffer a short period of cold to eliminate the bobcat that threatened his chickens. Warmed by coffee, Oneacre left the house two hours before sunup. At daylight he began blowing into his small plastic predator call. Although not so fetching as an electronic game caller, any approximation of a rabbit squeal was nearly irresistible to a hungry bobcat or coyote.

Applacha aptly headed towards the sound, showing only a modicum of caution. Hunger again outweighed wariness. At 80 yards, she stopped, sat on her haunches, and attempted to spot the dying rabbit. The ground blind of Oneacre blended in smoothly with the pile of rocks, and Applacha detected nothing of concern. The hungry coywolf began a slow stalk.

Oneacre spotted Applacha 65 yards away, a fairly easy shot given the scoped deer rifle he held. Using a small collapsible tripod, he set the crosshairs onto the coyote's left shoulder. With confidence, he began a slow squeeze of the trigger.

Leaving the blind the previous evening, Oneacre had stopped 50 yards away and urinated on the base of a serviceberry tree. Although quite faint in its snowy recession, the lingering odor was detected by Applacha. She suddenly stopped, and sidestepped towards a mountain laurel.

The gunpowder inside the brass of the .30-30 shell exploded as if synchronized with Applacha's turn, and the lead bullet split the thick hide covering her neck. Stung sharply, the coywolf raced out around the snowy mountainside. Oneacre swiftly worked the bolt-action rifle, ejecting the spent shell and loading a second. He had time for one shot but knew he had missed when he saw a puff of snow two feet behind his target.

Applacha did not stop until she reached the safety of Canaan Valley State Park. There she headed directly towards the cabin area and foraged around trash cans until she found three badly-burned hotdogs, enough to ease the hunger pangs.

Applacha made no more hunting trips to the Flanagan Hill area that winter. Her desire for sheep and chickens never returned. She started to alter her routine, hunting throughout the nighttime, sleeping a few hours in the morning, hunting again in the afternoon, sleeping again, and then beginning her nightly forays. Often covering as many as nine miles, she managed to find enough food to survive, although her weight continued to drop.

COYDOGS

In mid-February, Applacha worked her way around a string of beaver ponds on a tributary of Club Run. Unbeknownst to her, she was being trailed by two dogs. The hounds were not hunting dogs, although they were tracking Applacha's scent. She had entered estrus and had begun emitting a sex attractant. All members of the Canidae (dog family) are similar enough that the sex attractant given off by the female of one species will attract males of others.

Had Applacha lived with other coyotes, she would have been pursued by as many as nine or ten males. Applacha had not yet entered the reproductive stage where she would be attracted to a male coyote—if one had been present. If pursued, she would have run away, or aggressively attacked it.

Male dogs, both domestic and feral, have mated with female coyotes. The resultant offspring are labeled "coydogs." Similar to the interaction of a wolf and coyote, the male typically must be larger than the female for mating to occur. Thus, a male wolf would mate with a female coyote, or a large, male domestic dog would mate with a female coyote.

One of the hounds was a beagle, while the other was a cross between a blue tick bear hound and a German shepherd. The beagle, at 27 pounds, was dwarfed by the bear hound/shepherd, who weighed over 75 pounds. Applacha identified the hounds only when they were within 30 yards, and immediately fled at top speed.

The dogs continued their pursuit, but did not run or bark. Her sex attractant hormones were so powerful that their mating instinct overpowered their hunting instinct. The coywolf, sensing no attack, slowed her pace after a few hundred yards, and sat on her haunches. She watched curiously, as the hounds came within 40 yards, then galloped away.

The pursuit continued all day, and into the next morning. When Applacha stopped to rest or nap, the hounds also stopped, typically 20 yards away. After the third day, Applacha began to accept their presence. Her reproductive cycle was slowly progressing to the point where she would be attracted to a male—even a male hound.

One night Applacha curled into a ball, extended her bushy tail over her face, and closed her eyes. The beagle approached within two feet. When his nose lightly touched her rump she emitted an angry snarl, and pounced. Instinctively, she clamped her jaws around the cowering hound's neck. Before he had time to respond, his neck was broken. Before he could release a howl, he was dead. Thus ended Applacha's first courtship.

The shepherd hybrid remained curled up 15 yards away, watchful but making no move. Applacha ripped open the beagle while the shepherd studied her. After filling her stomach, she again curled into a ball and slept. That evening, Applacha again fed on the beagle while the shepherd watched. The two remained near the beagle carcass for another day, at which time the coywolf initiated a hunt. The shepherd trailed at a distance as Applacha stalked and captured three meadow voles.

On the fifth day, Applacha tolerated the close approach of the shepherd and on the sixth day she allowed him to push against her rump. Two days later they coupled, and fertilization resulted. As her sex attractant diminished, the shepherd remained with her, but began to lose interest. Three days after coupling, he headed back towards Red Creek.

A male dog is ready to copulate with any willing female canine, at any time of the year. By contrast, both male and female coyotes are sexually cyclical and capable of mating only during one period of the year—typically late winter. Males are sterile eight months of the year, and a female is nonproductive during ten months. Coyote males carry on a protracted courtship, domestic dogs in contrast, exhibit no such behavior.

Had Applacha mated with a male coyote, he would have become her constant companion, but the semi-feral shepherd had no such drive. Applacha would have no assistance in hunting, no assistance in selecting a den site, and no assistance in raising pups.

February, March, and early April were difficult times for the lone coywolf. As the pups within her grew, hunting grew ever more difficult. Deep snows allowed her to run down two yearling does during late winter, but otherwise she subsisted on nothing but meadow voles. She was losing weight, and by April weighed only 47 pounds.

As the 60-day gestation period inched closer, Applacha put the finishing touches on her natal den. She had selected an old groundhog den near the junction of Club Run and the Blackwater River, barely a mile from the park cabins. The burrow was nearly seven feet in length, ending in a relatively spacious den that was wide enough for her to easily turn around. It was important to have a den only slightly larger than she was, in order to maintain comfortable temperatures.

Red-winged blackbirds had returned from their wintering grounds as Applacha removed the last of the den's excavated soil. At about the same time, red maple twigs and buds were showing a slight reddish tint. A few weeks later, ramps had pushed their greenish leaves above the decaying leaf litter. Wood ducks and green herons were searching for nesting trees, as were barred owls and broad-winged hawks. Woodcock had returned from their southern wintering grounds and were engaged in nightly courtship rituals.

Applacha gave birth to four pups the second week of April. Three of the pups appeared healthy, although small. An underdeveloped female was stillborn. Applacha cleaned the three squirming pups and within minutes, they were nursing on her nipples. She sniffed at their unmoving sibling, nudging it repeatedly before suddenly grasping the pup, and following two firm crunching bites of its head, swallowed the slippery carcass much as she would a large meadow vole.

Applacha remained in the den with her newborn pups for 20 hours, intermittently nursing them before hunger drove her outside. She captured two small meadow voles, and returned to the skeleton of one of the yearling deer she had killed earlier. Although no flesh remained, she crushed the rib bones and swallowed the particles. Still hungry, she returned to her den and nursed her pups.

The life of a coyote is a daily struggle to kill and avoid being killed. Being a coyote mother is always a challenge, but being a single mother was especially challenging. A mate would have brought food almost daily while she was nursing her pups. And, as the pups reached the weaning stage, the male would have offered regurgitated food to them.

None of Applacha's pups reached the weaning stage. Two died when less than a week old and were eaten almost immediately by their famished mother. With all of Applacha's milk supply now flowing to the lone surviving male pup, it managed to survive. At four weeks of age, earlier than was typical, the stunted pup began following his mother into the den's burrow. He spent many hours at the mouth of the burrow, anxiously awaiting his mother's return from her nightly hunt.

Following her hunts on warm days, Applacha frequently played with her pup outside the den. One day she brought him the small leg bone of a groundhog, another day the dried foot of a rabbit. Often she would take the "plaything" from the pup, carry it a short distance away, and hide it in a clump of grass. If the pup tired of chewing on a bone, she would again carry it a short distance away and encourage him to search for it. Mid-day naps found the two curling up in close contact, much as Applacha and her father, Adirondus, had rested together. Reciprocal grooming was common during those events, and the bond between the two grew.

One evening when he was five weeks old, the pup ventured out of the den, curious and alone. His mother was on a nightly hunt. Applacha had started the weaning process a week prior to the time it would have normally occurred. She was having difficulty producing milk, and needed to reduce the demands on her body. The pup was searching for companionship that evening, but it was discovered by a soaring golden eagle.

The enormous raptor, its wingspan a full six feet, was using wind currents to maintain a steady glide. It had spent the winter in Canaan Valley, often gliding the full length of the valley in less than an hour before reversing direction.

The reddish-brown movement of the pup was detected by the eagle nearly a mile away, at an elevation of 4,000 feet. The eagle was nearly 700 feet above the pup when it folded both wings and dove earthward. Although the pup's eyes were capable of spotting an eagle at 500 feet, the coydog's focus was on searching for a bone or feather or insect to play with.

When 100 feet from the pup, the eagle was a blur plummeting 90 miles an hour, producing a faint bomb-like whistling sound. The coydog pup heard the sound, but did not shift its gaze skyward. Now 50 feet high, the eagle spread its wings to slow into a low-angle dive. The goal was to reach the pup while streaking only a few feet high, so that if it missed the eagle could pull up and soar safely upward.

The helpless pup heard the eagle as the majestic bird extended its legs forward and spread its yellow toes and three-inch long talons. A look of terror crossed the coydog's baby face, as he was snatched upward. The pup weighed a little over four pounds, but the eagle could easily carry eight pounds in flight. In that instant, the last surviving member of the first Canaan Valley coydog litter was no more.

Returning from her hunt the next morning, Applacha stopped at the mouth of the den burrow and emitted a low-keyed yip. She had captured a skinny groundhog that had emerged from hibernation recently. The scruffy-looking rodent weighed seven pounds, and provided Applacha with the first full meal in over two weeks.

When she received no response from the den, she dropped the groundhog and crawled into the tunnel. She was perplexed to find it empty. After crawling back out, she again called for the pup.

Hearing no response, she searched the area surrounding the den. She discovered a few drops of blood, but found no other sign of the vanished pup. She returned to the den, whined several times, and reluctantly crawled into the den where she spent the remaining daylight hours. As darkness fell, she returned and repeated the fruitless search for her pup.

Applacha abandoned the den the next day, and began roaming. April's second half brought green grass, ice-free beaver ponds, and the presence of Canada geese and groundhogs. May brought white-tailed deer fawns, goslings, young beaver and muskrats, wild turkey eggs, and many litters of meadow voles.

Applacha steadily regained weight and by June she was nearly 55 pounds. Her normal routine was to awake from sleep, stretch several times, urinate, and then emit a mournful howl! Every evening she listened intently for a response to her howl. But none came.

During summer, her home range spanned 20 square miles. The entirety of her home range was scent marked to announce to other canids that she claimed that particular parcel of land. Applacha regularly deposited urine on stumps, fallen logs, small boulders, and other prominent landscape features.

During early fall, she spent her early mornings in red spruce stands. Young red squirrels had abandoned their natal nests and were foraging across the forest floor. Not nearly as wary as their parents, the juveniles were an easy target for Applacha. She would lie in wait for a naïve squirrel to discover some food item. If a squirrel had ventured five to ten yards from a tree trunk when attacked, its future was in jeopardy. A juvenile red squirrel weighed only eight ounces, and Applacha needed at least ten to fill her stomach. Rarely did she catch that many.

Applacha also captured a few chipmunks, but she caught no gray squirrels or fox squirrels. There are no oak trees in Canaan Valley and thus no acorns—the food essential for gray and fox squirrels. The absence of oak trees in Canaan Valley is another of the ecological features that makes the area so unique and mysterious for ecologists, and so challenging for large predators.

Applacha's timber wolf DNA drove her to seek companionship, while her coyote DNA made her satisfied with solitary life. However, her size was a deterrent to killing a full-grown deer. Hunting season came, and again she benefited from an abundance of hunter-crippled deer and gut piles. At the end of January, Applacha began her second estrus cycle.

Early one February night, as the hunger moon made its appearance, Applacha awoke and shook off two inches of snow. Five inches of fat heavy snowflakes had fallen. Applacha had remained curled in a loose ball through it all, unable to hunt while the scent of potential prey was being buffeted in all directions. When the winds subsided and hunting conditions improved she began her nightly hunt.

A creature of habit, she tested the breezes for scents and sounds. The faint odors of a white-tailed deer wafted past her, but all thoughts of food were suddenly erased as the cold wind carried the distant howls of a coyote. As the howls ended, Applacha eagerly responded with a long howl of her own. A few yips were returned, but no more howls. With deliberation she began trotting towards the sounds. A visit to scent posts strategically positioned along the southeastern border of her territory would reveal the identity of the visitor.

Another annual reproductive cycle had begun for Applacha, and only time would reveal the outcome. Would she successfully raise a family of pups? Would she play a role in the extension of her lineage? Would a pack of coyotes/coywolves become established in the southern end of Canaan Valley? Could a female-led pack survive?

A small pack of coyotes/coywolves had been successfully established on the northern end of the Dolly Sods plateau by her father, Adirondus. Another had been established along the southeastern edge of the plateau by her sister, Estrella. Plenty of suitable territory remained for another pack to become established in the southern end of Canaan Valley. The Canaan Valley/Dolly Sods ecosystem could easily support three packs of coyote canids—one possibly led by a large, nearly black, female coywolf.

EPILOGUE

The coyote is now the most widespread of all North American carnivores and may well be the most widespread of all North American mammals. Moreso, it may be the only one currently expanding its geographic range into all available habitats. Today it is the most adaptable of all animals in North America.

Biologists generally agree that this mid-sized carnivore has been the most successful species in North America during the past 100 years. Not only has it endured the 90-year onslaught of private and government resources, but remarkably has thrived both in numbers and distribution during the same period. No wild animal has adapted to environmental changes as successfully as the coyote. It is an opportunist and a survivor without peer.

The late 1800s and early 1900s were a dark time for native North American wildlife, as many became extinct or neared that horrific level. Direct losses from hunting and trapping, plus indirect losses due to habitat destruction, occurred as humans expanded westward.

Some large animals were decimated by government-funded efforts. Bounties were paid by various governmental bodies, poisons were perfected, and private landowners employed whatever means were available. Wolves were a major target, but no other predator faced the type of war that was waged on the coyote. Livestock producers, especially sheep ranchers, believed they could not remain in business if coyotes continued killing their animals. Beginning in 1931, the U. S. Government employed hunters and trappers to remove the supposed threat posed by coyotes.

Government reports reveal that the USDA was responsible for the death of at least 80,000 coyotes yearly. All told, at least 400,000 coyotes were killed annually by governmental and private individuals. Government trappers killed an estimated six million coyotes between 1940 and 2000; private hunters and commercial trappers likely killed a comparable amount. State-employed trappers were surely responsible for the death of several million more. An estimated 20 million coyotes were killed during the 1900s.

Amazingly, by 2000, coyotes had expanded their geographic range to include most of Alaska, almost every province in Canada, every state in the continental United States, most of Mexico, and portions of Central America. No other wild animal on Earth has ever responded to such an all out elimination effort by actually increasing its numbers.

Part of the explanation for this unbelievable response is obvious in hindsight—the reduction of wolf numbers. Also helpful was an improvement in habitat quality and quantity for coyotes. Farming and logging inadvertently converted uniform, marginal habitat into optimal coyote habitat. Specifically, numbers and diversity of prey animals increased as a result of this landscape transformation.

The coyote's ability to adapt to humans and human habitats may also be unprecedented. Not only have coyotes adapted to every terrestrial habitat in North America, but they are utilizing backyards, cemeteries, golf courses, parks, roadsides, and various other habitats.

Coyotes are included in the order Carnivora—flesh-eaters. They are physically equipped to kill prey, even those larger than themselves. In fact, there are few, if any, animals that a coyote will not eat—both wild and domestic. Grasshoppers and cicadas (locusts), fish and amphibians (frogs and salamanders), reptiles (lizards and snakes), birds, and of course mammals, are all readily eaten. But coyotes also consume and digest a wide variety of plant materials. Numerous fruits and berries, plus many vegetables grown by humans, are dietary staples of coyotes. Melons, for instance, are a favorite. A coyote is not, to put it mildly, particular about what it eats. It may be the most omnivorous of all carnivores in North America.

Prior to European settlement of North America, coyotes were restricted to the prairies, including the southern tips of Alberta, Saskatchewan, and Manitoba, plus the small portion of northern Mexico located south of the Big Bend of the Rio Grande River. The main concentration of coyotes occurred within the area that would eventually become Colorado, Montana, Nebraska, New Mexico, North Dakota, South Dakota, Texas, Utah, and Wyoming.

In contrast, wolves (gray, Mexican, red, and timber) occupied much of North America. Coyotes were found only in the prairie region, which provided prime habitat for coyotes, but marginal habitat for wolves. Even there, coyote populations were marginalized by the occasional presence of wolves. Wolves killed coyotes! The coyote of the western prairies was considerably smaller than a wolf. Coyotes weighed 25-35 pounds whereas wolves weighed 90-120 pounds. And, because wolves typically ran in packs, coyotes had almost no chance to survive encounters with their larger cousin.

By 1900, as wolf populations declined, coyotes pushed north to Alaska, south through Mexico, and west to California. By 1990 coyotes had pushed to the Atlantic Ocean. Remarkably, this expansion occurred while *millions* of fellow coyotes were being killed through government sponsored, predator eradication programs.

Interbreeding between the smaller plains coyote and the larger gray wolf occurred as the societal structure of wolves was being fractured by humans. Any deterrents that had previously prevented interbreeding between wolves and coyotes began to break down as densities of both coyotes and wolves began to decrease. Male wolves mated with female coyotes, so that both size and behavior of the "new" North American canine changed. Whereas the plains coyote was inclined to be a solitary hunter, the hybrid coywolf hunted in small packs. They became capable of killing larger prey, especially deer. This new hybrid animal was an unforeseen outcome of human attempts to remove the two predators.

The early history (1950-1988) of coyotes in West Virginia was detailed by Jennifer Wykle in her Marshall University, M.S. Thesis, "The Status of the Coyote in West Virginia." She reported the first West Virginia coyote was killed near Davis in Tucker County in 1950. That female was positively identified by WVDNR biologists. During the 1970s, coyotes were reported from Fayette, Lewis, and Wayne counties. Sightings increased throughout the 1980s, and by 1990 they were common throughout West Virginia and were labeled as a serious threat to livestock.

The West Virginia DNR maintains detailed records of fur animals trapped and subsequently sold at annual fur auctions in West Virginia. The first coyote pelts appeared at the 1989-1990 auction, when five were sold. A total of 204 were sold in the 1990s, while 4,487 pelts were sold during 2000-2009. Total coyote pelt sales in West Virginia erupted to 19,804 during the 2010-2020 period.

Annual sales of coyote pelts from West Virginia auctions do not necessarily represent all coyotes killed. Some pelts may have been sold at auctions outside West Virginia, and, of course, some pelts are never sold at auctions. Fluctuations in pelt prices have accounted for some of this annual variability. The average annual coyote pelt price since the year 2000 has been slightly over $15.00, with a range from $9.26 to $19.46. The highest price for a coyote pelt brought $42.50 at the Glenville Fur Sale in March 2020. A single bobcat pelt brought $35.00, a fisher $27.50, a river otter $24.00, a beaver $19.00, and a mink $5.25.

Although a great diversity of plants and animals exists in Canaan Valley, it is not optimum habitat for coyotes. The one food considered by many biologists to be essential for maintaining a population of coyotes is rabbits, which are rare in Canaan Valley. Small populations of the New England cottontail and the snowshoe hare live on Dolly Sods, but are nearly nonexistent in Canaan Valley.

To my knowledge, no snowshoe hare has ever been reported in the Valley, and I, personally, have seen only two cottontails in nearly 50 years of conducting research within Canaan. However, cottontails are known at scattered locations in the southern end of the Valley—usually near gardens and lawns.

I have never seen the tracks of a cottontail in the undeveloped portions of Canaan Valley. The reason for this apparent anomaly is unknown. I can only conjecture that the scarcity of blackberries and raspberries plays a role. Thickets of such plants provide excellent escape cover for rabbits. Also, stems of blackberries and raspberries are an essential winter food for rabbits.

Coyotes will likely continue to roam Canaan Valley and Dolly Sods regardless of the scarcity of rabbits and hares. The key to their survival is plentiful white-tailed deer. As eastern coyotes become larger, through both interbreeding with timber wolves and naturally by living in a northern climate, they will get efficient at killing deer.

The presence of fawns during May will provide easily-obtained prey when coyote pups are being weaned and learning to hunt. Adult deer provide food for coyotes during the months-long hunting season as gut piles, wounded animals, and runaway kills are easily found. During January and February coyotes might cull some of the winter-weakened deer. Coyotes have a surplus of food available to them in Canaan Valley during spring, summer, and fall months, and are only stressed during late winter.

A critical balance of deer and coyotes must be maintained for both species to establish healthy populations. Deer numbers will eventually decline if coyote numbers increase beyond some currently unknown level. But likewise, coyote numbers will decline if deer numbers decrease significantly.

Many wildlife biologists believe a small population of coyotes would play a major role in maintaining the health of the Canaan Valley deer herd by addressing overpopulation and by removing unhealthy and diseased individuals. By preventing a serious overpopulation of deer, the overall health of the Canaan Valley ecosystem will be maintained. Keeping numbers in balance is a difficult task—especially when considering the attitudes of humans.

A key factor in determining whether coyotes will become permanently established in Canaan Valley is their social behavior. Single coyotes are unable to kill a healthy adult deer in winter. A pack, consisting of five or more individuals, has such capability.

Western coyotes have rarely formed packs similar to those of timber wolves. Rodents and rabbits (plus an occasional roadrunner) are the primary foods eaten by western coyotes, and they are easily killed by a single coyote. The eastern coyote, however, may eventually modify its social behavior to form small packs. Such a pack would probably include the alpha male and his mate, the previous year's litter, and the current year's litter. Such a social arrangement would become more likely if sexual maturity is delayed until individuals are two years old. Increased size of adults, which could occur because of occasional mating with gray wolves and the influence of colder northern climates, would be correlated with a delay in sexual maturity.

One of the key maxims of wildlife biology is "Nature abhors a vacuum." If there is an empty niche, i.e. that of a large (or moderately large) predator, it will eventually be filled. If not, certain prey species will increase in numbers to the level at which they cause harm to the vegetation of the area. An empty niche was produced when timber wolves and mountain lions were eliminated from the eastern mountains. If deer numbers remain high, the eastern coyote is the only large predator that can fill the niche of top, or "apex", predator.

The return of timber wolves to the central Appalachian Mountains is unlikely, because humans won't tolerate it. The return of mountain lions in numbers large enough to regulate deer numbers is also unlikely, because they will eventually attack a human as they increasingly encounter bikers and hikers. Black bear will continue to kill a few deer fawns, but they are in hibernation when adult deer are most vulnerable to predation.

For coyotes to fill the role of top predator, they must form packs, and whether humans will tolerate packs of coyotes roaming their mountains is not known. As numbers of human hunters continue to decline, coyotes could play a beneficial role in preventing an overabundance of white-tailed deer. But only if the public tolerates their presence.

It appears likely the howls of coyotes will become a fixture in our mountains and valleys. Based on coyote behavior in other states, this wily mid-sized carnivore will slowly adapt to humans, and it will become as firmly established in residential areas as is the white-tailed deer.

To summarize its current status in West Virginia, "C" is for coyote and canine and carnivore, and for canny and crafty and curious, and for calculating and callous and cunning, and certainly for controversial.

Appendix

The Most Infamous Coyote in West Virginia

The most famous, or infamous, coyote to live in West Virginia was in Upshur County in 1968. It began killing numerous sheep on various farms in Upshur County and neighboring Lewis County. More than 1,000 sheep were reportedly killed between late 1968 and early 1970. Over an 18-month period, and 165 square miles, the lone marauder paid visits to dozens of sheep farms. Strangely, it did not kill because of hunger. Most of its victims were killed but not eaten. He would crush a sheep's throat and esophagus but leave no other bite marks. It is highly unusual for any predator to kill for the thrill, but that appears to have been what this coyote did.

The serial killer coyote was slaughtering about 60 sheep per month during its reign of terror. That means it was killing two sheep per night—more than even a pack of coyotes could eat. Never were two coyotes seen together, nor were two single coyotes reported at widely separated locations. There is no evidence to indicate that more than one coyote roamed the area at that time.

One explanation proposed by a few biologists was that free ranging, feral dogs were killing the sheep. But no sheep farmer, hunter, or trapper ever reported seeing a pack of dogs in the area. No dogs were captured by professional trappers but at least 21 solitary "farm" dogs were shot by sheep farmers in their eagerness to kill the predator.

Local sheep farmers, hunters, and trappers had no luck finding the coyote. In frustration, they hired a professional coyote tracker/hunter from Kansas. He brought six of his prize hounds, but they failed even after extensive searches.

Helicopters and single-wing airplanes were also used with no success. Gus Douglass, Commissioner of West Virginia Department of Agriculture at the time, spent many hours in the front seat of a helicopter with the door removed and shotgun in hand, while cruising over Upshur County. He never got a shot.

The coyote was finally captured by Clyde Campbell, a West Virginia DNR trapper. For details of the capture see the newspaper article, *Killer Coyote Killed*, and the magazine article, *The Coyote That Outfoxed A State*, both reprinted below.

Killer Coyote Killed

from the *Dominion News*, Morgantown, West Virginia, 29 April 1970.

BUCKHANNON, W. Va. (UPI)

The howl of the coyote faded into legend Tuesday with a blast from a sheep farmer's rifle.

"Thank God, this is the end of this," muttered Charles Marple, after ending a long killing spree that cost sheepmen in Upshur and Lewis counties more than $20,000.

Marple found the coyote bleeding to death in a steel trap that he dragged more than 300 yards near Berlin, Lewis County.

Revenge was sweet for Marple, who lost 52 sheep last year and seven this year. He pumped two shots from a 243 Remington for good measure.

"Now I can turn my sheep out," he said referring to about 150 head on his 400-acre farm nearby.

But some of the blame or credit lies in the area of love.

Ginger, a nine-year-old coyote caught as a pup, had waited patiently in a trap-laden cage atop a mountain ridge for the coyote to give up murdering sheep for some romance.

He often came, noted State Department of Natural Resources information spokesman Bob Combs, but his sense of danger sniffed out carefully hidden traps.

Ginger heard the love howl often, but hunters and trappers gave up the idea about a week ago. They removed the traps and also some nesting used to make Ginger's outdoor stay comfortable.

That same nesting was used to conceal the same trap that finally snared the marauder Monday night.

"I think the smell of Ginger had something to do with it," Combs said. The fatal trap was set by Clyde Campbell, an Upshur trapping official.

After months of evading scores of angry sheep farmers, hunters, and even a professional tracker who brought six trained walking hounds from Garnett, Kansas, the pitfall of a simple machine seemed an anti-climatic way to go.

But the coyote, unwilling to let a score be evened, pitched a late-inning rally, and scooted his injured body and the 12-pound snare to the farm of Orville Long, where a fence entangled him.

And there he stayed until Marple happened along.

News of the kill ushered in a wave of relief among sheep farmers, who have lost more than 700 sheep since January, 1969, and 109 since January 14, (1970) when the resources department began to keep score.

"I was a little disturbed when I found out he (Marple) shot him, but after what he's been through, I can understand," Combs said, adding the animal would have been killed anyway.

Authorities took the coyote to the Lewis County Courthouse in Weston, where about 400 persons hastily gathered when Marple's conquest was learned.

Another big crowd was on hand at Upshur's courthouse in Buckhannon. While there, officials also took the Lone Marauder to Buckhannon High School for an examination by biology students.

Combs said the animal would be mounted by Clarksburg taxidermist John Casto, and returned for public exhibit at the resource department's French Creek Game Farm near here.

Over a 16-month period and a 165-square mile area, the animal had left a bloody trail. At times, residents claimed to have seen it but the coyote haunted farmers and frustrated their efforts to kill him.

Finally, the farmers pooled money and hired Joe Raymond, the Kansas professional, but unseasonable weather storms plagued him in the search.

Then came Ginger.

As for the lady, she is not without companionship. There is a third coyote in these parts—also a resident of French Creek Game Farm.

The Coyote That Outfoxed A State

By Richard Grimes, Outdoors Editor for the *Charleston Daily Mail*, Charleston, WV.

For 18 months hunters tried every trick in the book to catch the sheep-killing coyote, but nothing worked—until someone remembered sex.

The hunt soon accelerated into a struggle for survival, both for the men and their quarry. What began as a routine effort to collect a sheep-killing wild dog mushroomed into a wide-scale search-and-destroy mission, the target of which was one maverick coyote who had no business being where he was.

Spanning 18 months from late 1968 to the spring of 1970, the hunt for the outlaw coyote ran an incredible maze over the jagged terrain that stretches 80 miles between Route 20 and West Fork River in West Virginia, 165 miles in all.

For many of the men—sheep farmers whose pre-dawn-to-nightfall labors bring meager profits—it was a desperate race against time. Many of them lost—the coyote decimated their flocks.

No one knows this coyote's origin. Robert Combs of the West Virginia Natural Resources Department believes the animal was brought in as a pup, most likely from a western state. Unable to domesticate it, the owner probably released it in the hills. Most biologists agree that coyotes found in the East were transplanted as pups from their natural homelands beyond the Mississippi. In West Virginia, there are rarely four free-ranging coyotes at any given time.

Because wild prey in populated areas is scarce, a coyote in such a situation turns to domestic stock, though by choice he prefers mice, rabbits, birds, occasional young deer, insects, even fruit. Unlike a fox, which requires only one or two square miles, a coyote needs up to 20 square miles of hunting territory. And coyotes prefer hunting after dark.

The West Virginia outlaw chose to ditch doctrine on the last count. On at least two occasions farmers reported seeing him attack their flocks before nightfall. The brazen animal once killed in midafternoon, only 50 feet from a farmhouse owned by Charles Marple. In contrast, he was spotted several times during daylight hours mingling with sheep he would return to kill after dark.

Unlike most predators, this coyote frequently singled out the healthiest sheep to attack, rather than the old or sick. He ruthlessly slashed through flocks, killing sheep in his way with a chop at the jugular to reach an animal fleeing for cover.

Traps were used early in the hunt, but the coyote side-stepped them, covering them with debris, or left his droppings beside them as if in disdain. Easily traveling 20 miles a night, the animal roamed ridges, swam lakes and doubled back on his track to confuse his pursuers.

"I always had the uncomfortable feeling, the coyote watched us look for him," said State Agriculture Commissioner Gus Douglass.

Once, when Douglass was on the hunt with several others, they walked over a sewer pipe serving as a bridge. The coyote boldly darted from beneath and swam across a pond before anyone could react.

The trappers then tried hunting alone or in pairs in an attempt to surprise the coyote when he was sleeping off a meal. All they hoped for was one clean shot. One such trapper was Clyde Campbell of French Creek Game Farm, who suspected that the coyote, active the night before, might be sleeping atop the rock ledge of an abandoned strip-mine site. Campbell loaded his gun and took off for a hike of several miles.

Arriving at the base of the ledge, he climbed up, and near the top found the coyote asleep, oblivious to the world. In his excitement, Campbell rustled a bush. The coyote sprang up and zagged away as the trapper shot raggedly, then hopelessly.

Tracking dogs, primarily foxhounds, joined the hunt, but although they'd get hot on the coyote's trail for a moment or two, they would inevitably lose it amid deer tracks. The coyote would hear the dogs coming and join or fall behind a herd of deer. When the opportunity arose, he would angle away, usually where conditions precluded tracking.

Once, as dogs followed the coyote into a herd of cattle, an excited farmer mistook the dogs for coyotes and fired. Fortunately, he missed, but other dogs were not so fortunate—at least 21 were mistakenly killed by sheep farmers.

Only once did a foxhound make contact. Tracks in the snow showed where the coyote circled the dog several times and prepared to make a stand. The foxhound knew he was outclassed and fled.

A year passed. Sheep kills mounted. A study of tracks and the method of the kills convinced trappers they were looking for just one male coyote, since a female would have attempted to mate with a dog and would probably have been spotted running with one, her wariness overcome by her natural urges.

Farmers began to grow desperate as their flocks diminished. Committee meetings were held and rewards for the coyote's carcass grew as the months passed. State assistance was sought in late 1969.

With the first snow it was agreed that the hunt had to be intensified. Snow tracks would give the pursuers a considerable advantage. By early January of 1970 the hunt was being conducted on a daily basis. George Raymond, a Kansas rancher who owned dogs trained especially for coyote tracking, was brought in. Raymond used six registered Walker hounds that had been running coyotes since they were pups. The training showed. His pack responded to the coyote scent immediately and stayed hot on it long after other hounds became discouraged and quit.

Used to the flat Kansas terrain, however, Raymond's hounds encountered the same frustration as did the local dogs. Ultimately one of his prized Walkers disappeared, to be found a few days later—75 miles away, near the Ohio River, en route home. "Dot" had thought better of the maddening hunt.

Still, Raymond refused to give up. Calling on his years of coyote-chasing experience, he gave the search party a pep talk one cold dawn.

"That coyote," declared Raymond, "will stand on the next hill to see whether you've got a shotgun or a rifle and act accordingly. You're chasing a four-footed computer." The 20-persons in the party that day were to find those words accurate. The coyote showed himself just out of range, then melted into the woods.

Soon an air assault was launched against the coyote. The National Guard provided a helicopter and pilot and the Consolidated Gas Company of Clarksburg provided several helicopters and personnel. The

State Natural Resources Department chipped in land-travel equipment to supplement smaller aircraft.

For the first time permits to shoot from aircraft were issued. Planes flew as low as 50 feet above the ground instead of the usual minimum of 1000. Area radio stations WBUC in Buckhannon and WHAW in Weston—along with television stations WDTV in Weston—received numerous calls claiming airplanes had crashed, or at least were seen sinking just over a hill. Agriculture Commissioner Douglass tells the story of a farmer and his two sons who were spreading manure when a plane carrying Douglass roared up a canyon and over their heads. "As we looked back," says Douglass, "all we could see were the boys face down in the manure and the old man's feet sticking out from under the spreader."

Personnel at the state-operated French Creek Game Farm kept searching for some means of stopping the coyote. Well-meaning suggestions poured into State Natural Resources Department headquarters from around the country. An Ohio man recommended the use of simulated howls to lure the coyote. A letter from a Washington woman suggested traps with "heavy glue." Still another woman chastised the hunters for not using "love and kindness" to capture the outlaw.

It was now mid-April and the end of the chase was nearing. With all the modern equipment and techniques available, it would be the coyote's instinctive needs—his urge to mate—that would cause his capture.

As bait, NRD trappers brought in a caged nine-year-old female coyote two weeks into heat. She was placed atop a hill on the Orval O. Long farm in Lewis County where, in the words of a local newspaper, the Republican Delta, "she held court under the April moon."

But the coyote wasn't eager to let romance end his career. Tracks indicated he was approaching no closer than 30 feet to the cage. Then George Raymond got the idea of making the coyote think the hunters had left but the female hadn't.

Men opened the cage, collected the litter and spread it along fence posts leading to the trap area (the coyote was in the habit of slithering along fences). Litter was also sprinkled in the straw placed over several traps.

His incredible wariness dulled, the coyote approached the area along the fence about 2 a.m. on April 23. He stepped on the straw—and was down in a trap. For more than 300 yards the coyote dragged the trap and an anchor chained to it until the weight tangled in a barbed-wire fence. That morning farmer Charles Marple killed the coyote with a single shot through the heart.

So ended the chase that already had become a legend in the rural community where the coyote set a record for marauding.

The coyote had killed more than a thousand sheep with a value of about $75,000, and a like amount had been spent in the prolonged campaign against him. Thousands of man-hours were contributed. Farm dogs were shot in the belief that they were the elusive coyote.

The presence of this remarkable animal has not been lost, however. If your travels ever take you to the West Virginia foothills, stop off at the state-operated French Creek Game Farm where—right in the middle of the lobby—stands the mount of the maverick coyote. If you'll move in close and study his left eye you'll see there's an ornery twinkle in it.

** Published in *True Magazine*, February 1972.

BIBLIOGRAPHY

Books

Bekoff, M., ed. Coyotes: *Biology, Behavior, And Management.* Cambridge: Academic Press, 1978.

DeStefano, Stephen. *Coyote At The Kitchen Door: Living With Wildlife In Suburbia.* Cambridge: Harvard University Press, 2010.

Dobie, Frank J. *The Voice Of The Coyote.* Lincoln: University of Nebraska Press, 1947.

Ellins, Stuart R. *Living With Coyotes.* Austin: University of Texas Press, 2005.

Flores, Dan. *Coyote America: A Natural And Supernatural History.* New York: Basic Books, 2017.

Parker, Gerry. *Eastern Coyote: The Story Of Its Success.* Halifax: Nimbus Publishing Limited, 1995.

Reid, Catherine. *Coyote: Seeking The Hunter In Our Midst.* Boston: Mariner Books, 2004.

Ryden, Hope. *God's Dog: The North American Coyote.* Guilford: The Lyons Press, 1975.

Stockton, Shreve. *The Daily Coyote.* New York: Simon and Schuster, 2008.

Van Wormer, Joe. *The World Of The Coyote.* Philadelphia: J. B. Lippincott Co., 1964.

Way, J. G. *Suburban Howls: Tracking The Eastern Coyote In Urban Massachusetts.* Indianapolis: Dog Ear Publishing, 2007.

Young, S. P. and H. H. T. Jackson. *The Clever Coyote.* Lincoln: University of Nebraska Press, 1951.

Magazine Articles

Bonwell, Bill. "Coping With Coyotes." *Wonderful West Virginia Magazine* (1996).

Grimes, Richard. "The Coyote That Outfoxed A State." *True Magazine* (1972).

Murphy, Jody. "Mythbusting." *Wonderful West Virginia Magazine* (2019).

Scientific Publications

Albers, G. "Coyote Diets In West Virginia." 2012. M.S. Thesis, Morgantown: West Virginia University, (2012).

Albers, G., J. W. Edwards, R. E. Rogers, and L. L. Mastro. "Natality Of Yearling Coyotes In West Virginia." *Journal of Fish and Wildlife Management* 7: 192-197, (2016).

Bohling, J. H., L. L. Mastro, J. R. Adams, E. M. Gese, S. F. Owen, and L. P. Waits. "Panmixia And Limited Interspecific Introgression In Coyotes (*Canis Latrans*) For West Virginia And Virginia, USA." *Journal of Heredity* 108: 608-617, (2017).

Bozarth, Christine, F. Hailer, L. L. Rockwood, C. W. Edwards, and J. E. Maldonado. "Coyote Colonization Of Northern Virginia And Admixture With Great Lakes Wolves." *Journal of Mammalogy* 92: 1070-1080, (2011).

Crimmins, S. M., J. W. Edwards, and J. M. Houben. "Canis Latrans (Coyote) Habitat Use And Feeding Habits In Central West Virginia." *Northeastern Naturalist* 19: 411-420, (2012).

Houben, J. M., W. R. Bonwell, and T. R. McConnell. "Development Of The West Virginia Integrated Predation Management Program To Protect Livestock." *Proceedings Vertebrate Pest Conference.* Volume 21, page 70, (2004).

Mastro, Lauren L. "Life History And Ecology Of Coyotes In Mid-Atlantic States: A Summary Of The Scientific Literature." *Southeastern Naturalist* 10: 721-730, (2011).

Mastro, L. L., D. J. Morin, and E. M. Gese. "Home Range And Habitat Use Of West Virginia *Canis Latrans* (Coyote)." *Northeastern Naturalist* 26: 616-628, (2019).

Taylor, R. W., C. L. Counts III, and S. B. Mills. "Occurrence And Distribution Of The Coyote, *Canis Latrans*, In West Virginia." *Proceedings of the West Virginia Academy of Science* 48: 73-77. (1976).

Wykle, J. "The Status Of The Coyote In West Virginia." M.S. Thesis, Huntington: Marshall University, (1999).